This book is dedicated to
Val McCallum

ACKNOWLEDGMENTS

Val, Shelly, Katrina, Doug, Suzanne, Neal, Tony, and Charlie—
    our skiing companions on this project.

Celia Jensen—for her help in the preparation of this manuscript.

David McCallum—my computer doctor.

Bernard and Suzanne Lariviere—thank you for everything.

Joanne, Michele, Pierre—you guys are the best!

Victor Gerdin—the Ski School Director at Snowmass—
    for providing us with information about their excellent pro-
    grams.

Bob Hostage and the staff at Betterway Books.

CONTENTS

1.

TEACHING CHILDREN TO SKI

Welcome to the world of children and skiing! We hope that teaching your children to ski is a fun and rewarding experience for both you and your children.

It's admirable that you want to teach your children yourself. Too many parents are eager to unload their youngsters by enrolling them in day care centers, ski schools, and other programs for every moment of the vacation. Your children will probably enjoy their ski vacation a lot more since your entire family will be skiing together.

A child's youth is a relatively short period of time. Teaching your children to ski will provide you with the opportunity to spend quality time with your children. Life's pressures and responsibilities can make it difficult to spend quality time with your children at home. Even when you have time, your children may be tied up with homework, friends, and other activities. A vacation—especially a skiing vacation—is an ideal opportunity to devote time to your children. They will probably look back in future years and remember the time you spent skiing together with fond memories.

YOU AS TEACHER

Before you undertake the job of teaching your children to ski, there are a few questions you need to ask yourself.

Day one on the slopes.

Three sisters take a break to pose for a picture.

Are You a Good Skier?

Be honest about the answer. Are you a beginning, intermediate, or advanced skier? Can you ski a variety of terrains and conditions? Most importantly, do you understand the concepts behind skiing? Do you understand what makes the skis turn? Can you explain the theories behind the technique you are teaching? Can you accurately demonstrate each technique?

We understand that it isn't necessary to be an expert skier to teach beginning skiing. In fact, if you're a strong intermediate skier and have an understanding of the theory behind ski technique, you are probably well equipped to teach your youngsters.

However, if you're still struggling on the slopes, don't try to teach your kids. You'll most likely instill bad habits that will have to be unlearned later. What children learn during their first few days on the slopes is the foundation for all their future technique.

Are You Still a Novice?

If you're a novice skier, it isn't safe for you to teach your children by yourself. Do you have the skill and technique to catch an out of control five-year-old—pick him up at speed—and stop? A child may suddenly point his skis straight downhill for the thrill of the bomb (as we all have at times). However, an unexpected speed run can lead to disaster if you don't have the ability to safely catch the child and stop him. Yes, it's important to teach safety from the start. Yes, you'll teach them not to ski out of control. Yes, they'll do it once in a while anyway!

If your skiing is up to the task, it's not too much of a problem. Catch the child, have a giggle, tell him not to run away, and continue the lesson. The point is, you don't want to see your child heading for a collision with a piece of maintenance machinery and be unable to save him because you're a poor skier.

Are You a Good Teacher?

In addition to evaluating your skiing ability, ask yourself if you are a good teacher. Are you patient enough to teach skiing? Are you capable of explaining a particular skiing concept in an understandable fashion? While it's true that younger children won't sit still for long conversations on the slopes, older children often benefit from explanations. (There are specific examples of the different teaching styles needed for various age groups throughout the book.)

Teaching your child to ski should be fun for both of you.

You'll probably be surprised how fast your child will learn to ski.

Do you know the answers to the questions: What is the fall line? Why should you plan your line? Why is it important to unweight your skis before a turn? If not, you may want to take a few lessons yourself so you can understand and explain these concepts.

That said, rest assured that this book does contain all the theory you need to teach basic ski technique to your children. However, a book can't give you instant technique. If you don't understand—or can't clearly explain—basic ski technique, how will you explain it to your child in a fashion he can understand?

Okay, enough of the negative stuff. If you're still here, let's go teach your children to ski!

COMMON MISCONCEPTIONS ABOUT CHILDREN AND SKIING

There are actually quite a few common beliefs about teaching children to ski that are completely untrue. One of the most common ones goes something like this:

MISCONCEPTION #1

Lack of fear is one of the advantages that children have over adults when it comes to skiing. Since children aren't scared, they learn much faster than adults.

Well, it might be more accurate to say "some kids" aren't scared. Actually, contrary to what many experts claim, children can be terrified of the whole concept of skiing when first introduced to the experience. We have seen some children take to skiing from the word go—but we've also seen a lot of children who seemed positively terrified of the concept of skiing. For them, sliding down a slippery hill with a pair of foreign-looking boards strapped to their feet was akin to punishment.

How much exposure your children have to snow before you take them skiing may indicate how accepting they will be of the new activity. For example, a child who lives in Vermont has experienced snow. She is used to getting bundled up to go out in winter, has played in the snow, knows what it feels like, and may have already experienced some "ski-like" activity in the form of sledding and sliding down slippery hills. Conversely, a four-year-old living in southern Florida has probably never even seen snow, doesn't have any experience with cold weather, and isn't used to the constricting clothes required on the ski slope.

It is not accurate to blindly believe that all children are fearless when it comes to skiing. If your child hasn't seen snow before, spend some time at the resort playing in the snow before you take her up on the mountain. Imagine what it would be like if you had never seen snow before. Wouldn't you like to take a walk and experience the new environment before someone put a pair of skis on you and pushed you down your first run?

Misconception #2

Children don't get hurt as easily as adults when they fall—which is another reason children aren't as scared as adults when learning to ski.

Well, there is a lot of truth to the above statement since most children do tend to "go with" a fall rather than fight it. While an adult's fear of getting hurt may cause him to tense up during a fall —which increases his chances of injury—a child generally won't, which helps him avoid pulled muscles and broken bones. Also, children are a lot more limber than adults. This flexibility enables them to avoid many breaks since their limbs have a wider range of movement. However, don't fool yourself. If children fall on hard-packed snow or ice, it is going to hurt them!

Where you and your children go to ski also affects how much pain they may feel during a fall. For example, the western ski resorts often feature fresh powder or soft pack. Falling in these conditions can be a lot of fun. Conversely, icy conditions are common at some of the east coast resorts. If your children fall hard on an ice-covered hill, it's going to hurt them as much as it would you.

Don't assume your children are safe from injury or pain because they are young. In fact, we strongly recommend young children wear crash helmets to avoid dangerous head injuries.

GENERAL TEACHING CONCEPTS

Before you charge off to the mountain with your children, there are a few concepts we would like to introduce that will help simplify the process of teaching them how to ski.

Teach One Thing at a Time

It's important that you do not try to convey too much information at one time. Most children end up retaining very little when bombarded with a lot of instruction all at once. For example, it's better for your child to understand how to snowplow well than to "sort of" have an understanding of two or three different concepts. Generally, the best way to teach is to introduce one skill at a time and then practice the new technique until your child understands it. Begin to combine techniques after you have introduced a variety of skills over the course of a few days. In most cases, your child will combine techniques on his own. The bottom line is to *keep things simple*.

Teach What is Useful

This book contains information about what you should teach to ensure your children become safe, competent skiers. Our philosophy is to teach only techniques that are relevant and useful to the child beginning to ski. Try to avoid teaching things that have the potential of "cluttering up" your child's repertoire of skills.

Children have the ability to sort out physical skills by themselves. For example, your child will probably discover her balance point on her own. Don't interfere with the natural learning process by attempting to speed things up with a dazzling array of exercises that you feel will improve her balance. Generally, the best way for children to learn is to let them discover what works through experience. Naturally, you should guide them through the process ... but don't overcrowd them with too much information.

Pay Attention to Each Child

If you have more than one child in your family, it's possible they may progress at different speeds. It's easy to begin to pay more attention to the child who is progressing fastest since he may become more fun to ski with. Sometimes the more verbal child is also the more aggressive skier—the result being he ends up demanding more of your attention.

Ironically, the child who is the slower learner will probably need more direct one-to-one instruction. For example, one of your children may be learning at a slower rate because of an irrational

This child is well-equipped with brand-name gear.

Teaching your children to ski will provide you with a fun way to spend time together.

This young skier is discovering her balance point while skiing tree trails through the woods.

You will probably find that teaching your child to ski is a very rewarding experience.

fear of falling. Perhaps a younger daughter, for example, doesn't have as much experience in physical contact sports as her older brother. Make sure you pay equal attention to all your students and individually evaluate each child's needs on the slopes.

Keep It Fun

Keeping your lessons upbeat and fun can help to ensure your children look forward to their lessons and pay attention to you. Remember, you and your family are on vacation! Don't ruin it by becoming a disciplinarian on the slopes. If teaching your children isn't fun for either you or your children, put them in ski school and all of you will have a more enjoyable trip. Having fun while teaching skiing should be easy since skiing is such an enjoyable activity!

Keep in mind that the word "lesson" implies school ... which may turn some children off before they even see the mountain. So don't "teach" young kids in the traditional sense; have fun with them. For example, if they fall down—fall down yourself and make a joke of it—and then teach them how to get up. If they aren't finishing their turns, introduce a game to see who can make the longest turns. Tell them to try to point their skis uphill and then ski backwards for a moment, turning it into another game. The idea is that you'll get a lot more information into your children if you avoid assuming the traditional teacher/student(s) roles. There are specific suggestions in the chapter on games and drills.

Keep it Simple

Don't over-complicate the process of learning to ski. Most children's attention spans are fairly short when it comes to listening to long lectures. It's much more effective to simply show them what they should do rather than try to explain the course of action in advance.

"A picture is worth a thousand words" applies to teaching your children to ski. For example, rather than attempt to explain the intricacies of why one should edge the inside of the skis in a snowplow—just show them a snowplow.

Begin on Flat Ground

You'll make much faster progress during the first few lessons if you limit your children to fairly flat terrain. There should be a little

Skiing backwards in front of your child is a good way to give instruction while teaching basics.

Stick to fairly flat slopes while teaching the basics.

bit of a slope, but not more than a very slight grade.

The primary reason to teach on fairly flat ground during the first few lessons is that it is much easier to learn the basics on flat ground. Most ski areas have an area set aside for total beginners. Each "new skier's area" generally consists of a short shallow hill that's often not longer than two hundred feet. A poma lift or J-bar usually services the slope.

Use the new skier's area to teach your children to snowplow and glide. These novice slopes are specifically designed to help new skiers learn fast, which they won't do on a hill that's too steep.

Resist the temptation to take your children up the hill too early. Odds are they will lose control and be at risk of becoming injured from colliding with other skiers. Your children will probably love the idea of bombing out of control once they discover the sensation of speed, which is another reason to keep them on the bunny slopes until they have mastered a basic snowplow (and another reason for the crash helmets).

Some parents attempt to get a little skiing in for themselves while teaching the kids to ski. Don't do it. Either devote your attention to teaching your children or go skiing without them. If you try to get some recreational skiing in for yourself, you may be tempted to take your children further up the hill than is really necessary or safe. Wait until you've taught them the basics of stopping, turning, and traversing. Chances are your child will learn these basics within a few days.

One solution would be to put your children in ski school for the first few days of instruction; once they've learned enough to safely ski higher up the mountain, you can take them yourself. This will give you and your partner a chance to ski for yourselves and share the remainder of the vacation with the children.

Keep Them Moving

Most children have lots of energy and short attention spans. One sure way to cause a child to lose interest in the day's lesson is to spend a lot of time standing around. If you keep your children moving, it forces them to pay attention to their skiing. Conversely, if you stand around to admire the scenery, some children start to examine the possibility of clubbing their siblings with a ski pole.

Another reason to avoid long actionless delays on the mountain

These kids are well-equipped and ready to hit the slopes.

Skiing is a lot of fun for children.

is the temperature. Kids (and adults) get cold when they stand around in the snow and wind. It's a lot easier to keep them warm if you keep them moving. Most children want to keep moving once they've learned the basics of skiing.

For children, *speed* is the main thrill of skiing. Rather than inhibit their enthusiasm, encourage them to experience the joy and exhilaration of skiing fast. Don't let your students do anything dangerous, but don't overprotect your children either. Some parents worry far too much about their young ones hurting themselves from skiing too fast. Speed is a part of what skiing is all about. Let your kids ski fast if they want to—as long as it is under your control and guidance.

Tell Them When They Do Well

We know you know this already, but it's easy to forget while teaching your child something as involved as skiing. All adult skiers have bad days. Feeling cold, wearing ill-fitting boots, dealing with bad weather, waiting in long lift lines, and suffering from fatigue can all contribute to mental (and physical) preoccupation on the mountain. It's easy to become somewhat self-absorbed while skiing; especially if things aren't going well for you on a particular day.

Remember that children need approval from their adult role models. A few words of praise acknowledging their accomplishments can go a long way toward building confidence and pride. The result is they'll enjoy themselves a lot more and be more receptive to skiing.

Don't focus on negative problems. If your child is having trouble in some particular area, don't continually point it out. Instead, encourage him by noticing the positive aspects of what he's doing.

Try moving on to something else rather than continuing with something that isn't working. Attempting to "drill" a skill into your children will probably result in them, and you, leaving the day with a feeling of failure. Don't do it. It's better to keep the lessons positive by moving on.

Teach Them to Stop

Teach your kids how to stop from the very first lesson on. One of the primary fears new skiers have—and children aren't any different—is the fear of crashing into something (or someone) as a result of being out of control. The ability to come to a positive stop is one of the skills that gives new skiers a sense of confidence—not to mention the important safety aspect of regaining control by stopping.

We know this sounds obvious, but we've seen lots of children who could ski straight, turn, glide, skid, and bounce ... but who couldn't stop quickly. The primary problem was that most of these young skiers had learned to rely on falling over to stop (because it's fun), rather than automatically executing a snowplow or hockey stop. So, teach your students how to safely stop from the word go. Falling over is a good way for children new to skiing to stop when they are out of control but don't let your children rely on falling. It will not always be a safe alternative. Make sure they develop a solid technique as well.

Learn to Recognize When Your Children Are Stressed

One of your jobs as a ski instructor is to recognize when your students are experiencing anxiety on the slopes. Often the cause of their fear or discomfort may be easily removed once you have identified the problem. You may be surprised to discover what's causing your child's anxiety. For example, we know of one young skier who consistently fell apart every time he was taken into the woods. The child would often begin crying at the mere mention of skiing in the trees; his fears seemed completely irrational. However, a little questioning revealed that the young skier was scared of encountering large animals such as bears while skiing in the trees. It seemed that a friend had told him that large child-eating animals lived in the woods. A few explanations later and the four-year-old was happily skiing the tree trails. Spend some time questioning children who seem apprehensive and try to discover the source of the problem.

Another cause of stress during the lesson could be you. Is it possible you are pushing the child into an activity she isn't ready for? For example, you may feel your child is ready to ski a black diamond run, but she may be terrified by the idea. It may have nothing to do with logic or reason — your child may simply be scared of any run that is labeled "expert." Often the best solution to these situations is to listen carefully when your child offers you an explanation. A lot can be discovered through listening to what your students tell you.

Don't Teach if You Are Feeling Impatient

We all have bad days. Fights with our spouse, financial worries, job concerns, physical ailments, or simply being hungry can all contribute to a lack of patience. Teaching children to ski requires a great deal of patience. If you are feeling burned out and edgy you may want to take the day off. One solution may be to let your spouse (or skiing partner) take over the teaching duties for an afternoon. It doesn't mean you are a bad teacher—or parent—we all need to take a day off once in awhile.

Don't Make Comparisons Between Children

The last thing a child who is having trouble wants to hear is how great his brother or sister is doing. A child definitely doesn't want to be told that he isn't doing as well as the other children in the group. We realize you would never intentionally put one child down over another, but it is possible to make comparisons that accidentally convey this message.

If you want to show a child the correct way to edge his skis, don't tell him to observe a sibling who is doing it right. The child may feel bad that he is not performing as well as his sibling, which could affect his performance and make him blind to the point you are trying to make.

A much better solution would be to use yourself as the example. Don't state that the child is doing anything wrong. As previously stated, it's much more effective to teach through physical example than through verbal explanations.

Review Your Teaching Ability

Mentally review your teaching style at the end of the day. Did your children have fun? Were you too strict? Are you teaching them solid skills? What can you do to improve the day's lesson? How many runs did you take with them? Did you see improvement?

Reviewing your lesson is particularly important if you're having trouble teaching your children. You may discover the solution to a particular problem once you're off the slopes and your mind is clear.

2.

SAFETY

Part of your job as your children's ski instructor is to ensure that they are safe while skiing. Children are generally unaware of the consequences of a given action if they don't have experience in a particular area. Your child has never collided with a 200-pound adult traveling thirty miles an hour on skis. An adult can imagine the consequences of a high-speed collision ... a child can't. In addition, most adults have experienced an array of painful injuries and thus are much more cautious about activities that could result in injury.

Many children love to point their skis straight downhill and blast to the bottom. So it's critical that you instill proper *risk awareness* from the first lesson. We feel so strongly about this that we have devoted an entire chapter to the subject of safety.

BINDINGS

Your children's ski equipment should have a thorough pre-season checkup before you let them hit the slopes. A child's weight may change considerably between ski seasons. It is also not uncommon for some children to grow several inches in a year. What may have been a safe and reliable din setting on your child's binding last year may be completely unsafe for the new season. We saw a child's ski come off in mid-air a few weeks ago. The resulting

Be sure to provide your children with a way to keep their faces warm to avoid frostbite.

Always provide your children with sunglasses or goggles to protect their eyes from the sun and wind.

crash didn't look fun. When Christine went over to help the child (who was alone) retrieve her ski, it was apparent that the binding's din scale was set too loosely since the ski could be pulled off the girl's foot effortlessly.

Don't attempt to adjust these bindings yourself. Take your child's skis to a professional ski shop and let a trained technician do the work. Another point to remember: don't hand down an older child's skis to a younger sibling without having the binding's din scale adjusted for the younger child's weight and ability. Obviously, a binding that won't release during a fall is a disaster waiting to happen.

OTHER EQUIPMENT

Ski Boots

Ski boots should also be checked pre-season. Children's feet can grow considerably in between seasons and boots that fit well last year may be dangerously small this season. Remember, a boot that is too tight can cut off your child's circulation and cause frostbite. If a child's foot becomes numb from an ill-fitting boot, he may not feel the early warning signs of cold feet. Make sure you consult your child about the boot's feel and fit at the start of the season.

Another consideration with ski boots is that the buckles may need to be set at different tensions from one season to the next. For example, if your child's ski boots are hand-me-downs that were a little large last year, but fit this year, you probably won't be setting the boot's buckles as tight.

Another safety consideration on the slopes regarding boots is to make sure there is no snow packed inside your children's ski boots when they go inside the lodge. A common scenario is the children's boots fill up with snow while skiing in powder. Then you go inside the lodge—where you unbuckle your children's boots to warm their feet up. The snow melts and your children's socks become soaking wet (as does the boot's inner lining). The danger here is that when you go back outside their feet will freeze.

The solution? First, check inside your children's boots for snow when you come into the lodge. Also, dry out wet boots and socks with whatever heat source is available while you are having lunch. Make sure that they do not put wet socks back on. It is better to miss a little time on the slopes while waiting for equipment to dry than to have anyone suffer frostbite.

Long Scarves

Long scarves should be avoided, as should any piece of clothing that is too big for or hangs off your child. The danger is that your child may become entangled with ski lift apparatus. We've heard stories about people being killed because their scarves became tangled up in a chairlift and strangled them. In fact, some ski areas have banned long scarves altogether for this reason. We recommend you don't allow your children to ski with anything around their necks that could endanger their safety.

Ski Poles

Ski poles seem to represent swords and spears to some children. Obviously, you must discourage children from "fencing" with each other with their ski poles. Also, "pin the tail" of another child with a ski pole and other similar activities should be discouraged. We know this sounds obvious, but we've witnessed more than one child clubbing another with a ski pole on various occasions.

Another concern with ski poles comes from other skiers besides those in your family. Point out that it's not prudent to stand too close to the person in front of you while waiting in the lift lines. People's ski poles sometimes slip backwards in a stabbing motion as they push forward. A small child is closer to the ground and thus more likely to become injured by a wayward pole.

HANDLING EMERGENCIES

Teach your children how to recognize the ski patrol personnel. Older children can also be shown what the emergency phones look like and where they are located on the mountain. Explain to them what to do if another child they are skiing with becomes injured and what to do if they come across an injured skier.

Ski areas are often extremely large and your children could become lost if left alone. While this shouldn't be a problem with older children and teenagers, younger children clearly shouldn't be left on the mountain unsupervised. Naturally, all the usual precautions about not talking to strangers who may approach them for no

Teach children to recognize the ski patrol.

Show your child how to recognize where emergency phones are located on the hill.

reason should be reinforced before children are allowed to ski by themselves.

It's important to teach your children what the various symbols and signs on the mountain stand for. While you understand that a double black diamond run is for expert skiers only, your children won't unless you tell them. Sit down with your youngsters and go over the ski area's trail map before you allow them to go off by themselves.

Some of the signs your child should be able to recognize are:

❑ trail difficulty indicators

❑ slow skiing area

❑ route down

❑ least difficult way down

❑ danger

❑ ski patrol

❑ closed—do not enter

❑ emergency phones

❑ clinic/emergency aid

❑ caution—blind skier

Having the ability to recognize these symbols will help ensure your children's safety on the slopes. Incidentally, you won't need to explain what these symbols look like ... they are generally pictured on the resort's trail map so you can simply show them to your child.

While not critical to their safety, you may want your children to know how to locate and identify the symbols that will lead them to the restaurants, kid's ski trails, nature trails, children's race area, warming huts, ski school meeting areas, child care facilities, and NASTAR race courses. It's important that they can identify the race courses to avoid accidentally skiing onto one while it's in use.

COMMON SENSE AND COURTESY

Some other general concepts that may seem like common sense to you need to be explained to younger skiers. Here a few that you should make sure your young skiers understand:

1. *Don't ski too near other skiers who have stopped on the mountain.* Teach your children to give a wide berth to people who are standing still on the slopes. You don't want your child skiing too close to somebody who may not hear him approaching. This could easily lead to disaster and injury.

2. *Yield to faster skiers.* Some children may instinctively want to race anyone who passes them. Explain to your child that he should yield to faster skiers. We've seen a few accidents on the mountain that were caused by a young novice skier crossing the path of a faster skiing adult. Illustrate to your child while the two of you are skiing how important it is to always *look uphill before moving across the slope*. A good way to demonstrate the danger is to point out a fast skier who is coming down the mountain in a fairly straight line. Explain to your child how easy it would be for a collision to take place if he were to cut across the skier's path unexpectedly. (Since this is similar in principle to looking both ways before you cross the street, it should be fairly easy for even the youngest skiers to grasp.)

3. *Don't stop where you can't be clearly seen.* Clarify to your children the importance of stopping only in areas where approaching skiers will be able to see them. The landing area of a jump and "blind corners" are not good places to stop, as approaching skiers will not be able to see them until it is too late to stop. One way to point out the danger is to stand and observe the landing area of a jump. As you watch a large adult land after a jump, ask your children to imagine what would happen if any of them were lying in the snow at the bottom of the jump as the adult landed.

4. *Maintain control.* We are all guilty of this one. Children, like some adults, are extremely fond of throwing technique out the window in favor of a high speed thrills. Although bombing is a lot of fun, your children are at greater risk of injury when they

are out of control. Explain to them that the risk isn't just from falling—which they may not fear—but from colliding with another out-of-control skier. Try to stress the fact that one of the ways to identify good skiers is that they are in control. We've found that this is often the hardest aspect of teaching children to ski. Some kids simply become speed freaks and refuse to accept the concept of turning or stopping. If necessary, take some form of mild disciplinary action to break this habit since it can easily end in disaster.

IF YOUR CHILD GETS LOST

Discuss what you and your children will do if any of them get lost on the mountain. Predetermine where your children should go to wait for you if they become lost. Naturally, only you can judge how much independence your children are capable of handling. Keep in mind that "lost" is a relative word when skiing on a large mountain. Most skiers spend a good percentage of the day "lost" if they are new to a ski area.

Perhaps the best course of action would be to give your child a predetermined time to meet you. Explain to them that although the family is going to rendezvous at 3:30, it may take them an hour to get themselves to the particular part of the mountain that has been designated as your meeting point. As previously stated, make sure your children understand how to read a trail map and/or seek assistance from the proper personnel. Discourage your children from asking total strangers for directions since it impossible to know who they may be dealing with.

It's always a good idea to send your children out with at least one other child if they are not under adult supervision. If you are a single child family, consider vacationing with another family who has children, or putting your child in ski school when you want to ski alone. Keep in mind that you are not going to want to teach your child 100% of the time. Odds are you and your spouse will want to go and get some recreational skiing in for yourselves.

Observe Your Children's Skiing Etiquette

One of the best ways to see how safe your children are when skiing alone is to observe them without their knowing it. Children may exercise completely different behavior patterns while supervised than when left unattended. We are not suggesting you breathe down your children's necks while they are skiing, but keep in mind that a high speed collision can be very dangerous. It is in the best interest of your children for you to do everything you can to instill good safety habits and risk awareness into their skiing education.

SKI LIFTS

The first time your child rides a chairlift, you should take some special precautions to ensure his safety—particularly if he is young. Most ski areas have a run that is designated for new skiers. The longer ones are usually serviced by a chairlift, while the shorter ones may have a poma lift or a J-bar.

The chairlift operator will slow down the lift and assist your child into the chair if you indicate that you have a young child who is new to skiing. All young children need to be lifted onto the chair since they are incapable of getting on safely by themselves.

Once you and your child are sitting and the chair is past the housing, pull down the safety bar and instruct your youngster to hold on to either the center or side bar. *Don't allow young children to sit on the edge of the chair.* It's much safer to place young children against the back of the chair, even if this means their legs can't bend. If a four-year-old sits on the chair in a fashion that allows his knees to bend (skis hanging down), chances are he will be sitting dangerously close to the end of the chair. This increases the possibility of his sliding under the safety bar and out of the chair.

As you approach the unloading area, indicate to the lift operator that you have a child who is new to skiing. The lift operator will slow down the chair so you can safely remove your child. Don't assume that the lift operator will automatically slow down the chair when you get on or off—especially if your child isn't that young. Always indicate to the lift operator that you need assistance. Sticking to the novice slopes and lifts will help ensure that you receive the needed attention.

If you opt to use a poma lift, there are two ways you can go. One method involves riding the lift with the child, holding both the child and the poma in front of you. This is awkward at best since you have to bend fairly low to hold the child.

Crash helmets are a good idea.

*One way to ride the poma lift with a new skier
is to hold the child in front of you.*

Another method often used since lifts of this type are usually fairly short on the novice runs is to run alongside your child as she takes the lift. The idea is that you can give instructions during the ride. We have found this method to be the best since you don't really need to wear your skis during the first hours of instruction. Once the child has mastered riding the lift, you can start riding behind her.

You may also encounter a T-bar or J-bar on the novice slopes. Riding a T-bar with a small child is difficult due to the fact that the bar will rest behind your knees if it is placed behind a four-year-old's butt. One solution is to hold the bar and the child in front of you while you both ride up. In other words, treat it like a poma lift. Same thing for a J-bar. Generally, most children are capable of riding poma, T-bar, J-bar, and rope-tow style lifts by themselves right away. You'll probably only have to offer assistance if your child is very young.

3.

EQUIPMENT

Children's ski equipment isn't very different in design from that used by adults. Skis, boots, binding, clothing, and other equipment all come in a wide variety of styles, colors, and price ranges. One of the best ways to get an idea of what's available is to go to one of the annual ski shows that take place in most major cities. Visiting a ski shop is another excellent way to get a feel for what is available; however, many stores conveniently favor brands that they carry. Whatever you decide, it's often better to buy complete packages made up of skis, bindings, and boots since most stores offer package deals on children's gear.

COST

One of the first questions you must ask yourself is: How many children will be using the equipment? For example, if you have four youngsters in your family, the ski equipment will most likely be handed down over the years. If this is the situation, you'll benefit by buying good quality equipment that will hold up over the years.

Conversely, if you only have one child, you may get away with less expensive equipment since the child will be outgrowing some of it fairly rapidly. However, do not compromise safety for price.

An option, especially if you have only one child, is to rent equipment for the entire season. Most ski shops located near major resorts have special deals on children's rental equipment. The standard package rate seems to be about $75.00. This provides skis, bindings, boots, and poles for the season. How long is a season? Many shops will offer this deal from November through April. Not bad . . . especially, if your child will grow out of the equipment by the next season.

The disadvantage of rental equipment is that it is often extremely beat up. With younger children, this may not be a problem since they are just beginning to learn to ski and don't need high performance equipment. As your children progress, however, you may want to invest in new equipment that won't hinder their ability.

The prices given in the following text are high end prices. With children's ski equipment, it's always possible to find something at a cheap price. Youngsters grow and parents sell the used equipment. There's also a lot of cheap new equipment on the market, although some of it is of fairly low quality. Once again, how much you invest depends on your child's ability, age, what you can afford, and how many children you have. It is very important, however, that you do not compromise safety for price.

SKI STYLES

Before you buy skis, it's a good idea to become familiar with some basic ski features and the intended function of different types of skis. Skis are usually named after the type of skiing they are styled for. The more common categories are listed below.

If your child is in the four- to six-year-old range and is just starting out, you won't need to worry too much about the type of ski you buy. The Blizzard Junior comes in lengths as short as 70 cm and 80 cm. This is a high quality ski about two feet long; it costs roughly $100.00. Yes, that's expensive for a young child's pair of skis, and yes, you can find them for less. However, skis in this price range will last through several children.

For older children and young teens, you should buy skis that are matched to their ability and style of skiing. Basically, it's just like buying skis for yourself.

Novice

Also called learner skis, this category is designed with the total novice in mind. Usually, skis in this group are slightly wider to provide increased stability during the first few hours on the slopes. Prices are in the $250.00 range.

We recommend you rent skis of this type for your children because they will most likely outgrow the skis (ability wise) within the first season. Keep in mind, we are talking primarily about older children and young teens here. The type of ski used is not really relevant for four- to six-year-old children.

Recreational

Recreational skis, as the name implies, are styled for general all-around skiing. If your child has a good grasp of the basics of skiing, say after the first season, then you may want to invest in a pair of skis of this type. Recreational skis are not a good choice if your child likes to ski fast or appears to be learning at a rapid rate. If this is the case, you may want to continue renting or buy better skis. Price for recreational skis is generally around $300.00 or less.

Sport

This is really just another version of the recreational ski. As with recreational skis, sport skis may be a good choice for your child's first pair. Cost is also about $300.00, often less.

Slalom

Now we are getting into mid-performance and high-performance skis. Just because a child is young doesn't necessarily mean he should ski on equipment of lesser quality than the accompanying adult. Many children begin serious training in pursuit of competitive-oriented goals as young as ages twelve or thirteen.

Slalom skis are designed for fast and easy turning on hard-packed snow. Many skis in this category are high end, high performance, and high price. Cost is in the $300.00 to $600.00 range.

Some slalom skis are designed for children with intermediate skiing ability. Naturally, these cost less than skis styled for people with a high level of skill. We recommend you buy your child slalom skis because they are generally easier to turn than stiff downhill skis. Slalom skis can be used comfortably in a variety of conditions, some other skis can't. For example, your child will be able to ski clumpy powder on a steep run after a couple of days of snowfall on her slalom skis (although there are better choices). Try the same run on a stiff pair of downhill skis that feature very little sidecut (more on that later), and she will most likely have a difficult time.

Giant Slalom

Giant slalom skis are designed for high speed. Although they are easier to turn than the pure downhill skis, giant slalom skis usually aren't as "lively" when initiating a turn as a slalom ski. Unless your child has strong intermediate to advanced ability, she is probably better off with a standard slalom ski.

We feel that some skis that are harder to turn can create bad habits with children who are not yet proficient on the slopes. What happens is the kids "adapt" in whatever way necessary to make the ski turn, often at the expense of their form and technique. For that reason, we recommend that you do not put your children on skis that are rated far above their ability. Prices range from $150.00 to $450.00.

Mogul Skis

More than likely you will be buying a set of these for your young adult. While many older skiers tend to avoid skiing the bumps all day, kids seem to thrive on it. Mogul skis are designed to be used in the bumps and are usually softer than other styles of skis to help absorb impact. Skis in this category are also high-performance skis designed for people who are fairly proficient in their technique. Prices are in the $300.00 to $600.00 range.

Downhill

High speed, stable, fun, and fast basically sums up the downhill concept ... children love it. Downhill skis aren't as easy to turn as slalom skis, but are a lot more stable as your child's speed picks up. Generally, don't buy downhill skis for your kids until they are at least intermediate skiers. Cost is comparable to that of slalom skis.

All-Terrain

If you and your family only go skiing once a year for a week-long vacation, this may be the type of ski to buy for your children. As the name implies, these skis will perform well on a variety of terrains and in a variety of conditions. They are designed for the intermediate recreational skier. Usually, all-terrain skis are fairly easy to turn and are forgiving of mistakes. Prices are usually in the $300.00 range for young children and can cost as high as $600.00 for teenagers.

Powder

Powder skis are wider and shorter than other skis and are fairly specialized. There is no reason to buy your child a pair of powder skis unless he is a good skier and skis in powder often. It's really a question of cost. Your children will probably not use their powder skis that often, but they are a pleasure to use when skiing in deep powder. Cost is usually fairly high, about $450.00.

Light Expert

Skis in this category are often ideal for children who ski well. Light expert skis are designed for people who are fairly good skiers and weigh less than 130 pounds. One of the primary differences between these skis and the "standard" models is that these skis are softer. The result is they're easier for a light person to turn. Put a child on a stiff ski designed for a heavy adult and she may find the ski unforgiving and hard to turn. The solution is to put her on a softer ski in this category. Cost is generally in the $300.00 to $600.00 range.

SKI FEATURES

Before you go out to buy (or rent) skis for your children, it will be helpful for you to become familiar with some of the terms salespeople use when discussing skis. Understanding the concepts behind ski design can go a long way toward picking a ski that is right for your child. Some of the more commonly used terms are:

"Why did mom put these on my feet?"

Make sure the equipment you buy for your child is easy to handle on the slopes.

Sidecut

How much sidecut a ski has relates to how it turns. Skis with a lot of sidecut are easier to turn than skis without much sidecut. A ski's dimensions are usually stated somewhere on the ski. Comparing these numbers will tell you if a particular ski has more or less sidecut than another model. Generally, you want to put your child on a ski that is easy to turn so it won't hinder the learning process. Once again, we are talking about older children and teenagers.

Camber

Skis are cambered, or bowed, to distribute the skier's weight evenly along the ski's length. Put a pair of skis together with the bottoms facing each other, and it will be easy to see the camber. Children, because they don't weigh much, don't need excessive camber in their skis. If it requires excessive weight to compress the ski, it may not be right for your child. Of course, this all relates to how much your child weighs. If your son is a 180-pound fifteen-year-old, he can be on the same skis as an adult.

Flex

A ski's flex can be felt by grasping the ski around its middle and then pulling the shovel (the front of the ski) back. A stiff ski will resist this flexing while a soft ski will be easy to flex. Flex describes how resistant a ski is to bending along its length.

Soft skis are probably what your child will need. Stiff skis are generally used for skiing at high speeds or by people who weigh more than most children.

Keep in mind that ski selection is related to how much your child weighs. As the young skier grows—and his weight increases—you will start to buy him adult skis that are designed for light people.

Ski Length

How long should your child's skis be? A good rule of thumb is to put your children on skis that are about six inches longer than they are tall. The thinking here is that your children won't outgrow the skis immediately. If you put your children on skis that are too short, they will inevitably start to "skid" their turns. Longer skis help ensure children will learn to carve their turns.

Skis have other features in addition to those discussed above, but they are not as relevant to children since children don't weigh as much as adults. Generally, if your child is in the seven- to twelve-year-old age category, look for a fairly soft ski that is easy to flex. Naturally, there will be exceptions — primarily if you are teaching a skier of above-average ability.

BINDINGS

Bindings for four- to six-year-olds generally can be found for about $75.00 to $90.00. As with the skis, this price buys "real" ski equipment. There are some cheap bindings out there but we recommend that you go with the name brands such as Marker or Solomon (there are others as well).

Older children can usually be put in bindings for about $100.00. Once a child is about ten years old, expect to pay about $250.00 for a pair of skis equipped with good quality bindings.

One of the first questions the salesperson will ask is how much your child weighs. Cost of bindings is somewhat dictated by the weight range they are designed to handle. Obviously, this in not a big consideration with young children but it can be for teenagers. For example, Marker makes some excellent bindings for lightweight people — less than 130 pounds — that cost about $130.00. However, if your teenage son is on the high school football team and weighs 200 pounds, you're going to need to purchase a binding that is rated for his weight range. Cost can be over $200.00.

Din Scale

A binding's din scale is used to set the binding to a skier's specific weight and ability. A ski binding must be a designer's nightmare. It has to hold a child's foot to the ski as she bounces over a variety of terrains but release the foot from the ski when excess pressure is present. Be sure to check that your child's binding isn't set too high. To do this, have your child raise her leg to the side and kick the front inside edge of the ski into the snow. Her foot should be released sideways at the toe piece. If your child can't kick out of the ski in this fashion, the din scale is set too high.

To test the heel release, have your child step into only one ski

... then stand on the back of the ski and have her take a step forward with her free foot and instruct her to try to "walk" out of the binding. A caution here: Don't let your child force the release if the din scale is set too tight since this can result in a knee injury. If the binding doesn't release easily, it's probably set too tight.

Make sure the bindings you buy are easy to operate. Some bindings are so simple that a four-year-old can step in and out unassisted. Other brands require "adult-like" strength to set. If you have a couple of children, all with equipment that is difficult to operate, you probably won't have a good time on the mountain.

Manipulate the binding in the store with your child. Can she operate it by herself? Is it difficult for you to operate? If you are having trouble in the store, imagine what it will be like on the mountain when your hands are cold. This concept of easy-to-use equipment should be kept in mind with everything you buy for your children.

Have your child's bindings serviced once a year. It's a small price to pay to ensure the binding will release when it's supposed to. Don't hand down used equipment to other children without first having it thoroughly checked by a qualified technician.

SKI BOOTS

Ski boots are another area in which you want to ensure ease of operation and a pre-season checkup. If your child is young, you may want to rent ski boots for the first few seasons since he will outgrown them rapidly. Ski boots for four- to six-year-olds cost about $80.00 and are of good quality. Both Nordica and Solomon make a variety of models for young children.

As previously stated, make sure the boots are easy to operate. We recommend a one-buckle design for young children.

Older children and teenagers have a much wider range of boot styles to choose from. Prices range from $100.00 to above $500.00. Obviously, the upper-end price range is for teenagers of expert ability. Some of the features you should discuss with your child and the salesperson before purchasing are:

How many buckles does the boot have?
Multi-buckle designs offer more adjustment options, while rear-entry single-buckle designs are generally easier to use. This is

a matter of personal preference that should be decided by each child. Fit and comfort should be the basis for the decision. Some children may need a multiple buckle design to obtain a comfortable fit.

Can the boot be adjusted in different ways?

Some skis boots can be adjusted in a multitude of ways; others offer only one buckle. Naturally, a boot's price often reflects how adjustable it is. Some of the more common adjustments found are:

1. *Forward Lean Adjuster* — which allows the user to set the amount of forward pitch on the boot.

2. *Cant Adjuster* — a cant is a wedge that is used to adjust the boots of a person whose legs aren't perfectly straight. A cant adjuster is a mechanical device in the boot that does the same thing.

3. *Arch Adjustment* — as its name implies, this allows you or your child to adjust the height of the boot's arch for more comfortable support.

4. *Heel Elevator* — some boots allow the heel section to be raised or lowered.

There are a host of other devices you may encounter, some of which are terrific, and some that are known as "dial-a-pain" adjustments. The important thing is to get your children involved in the selection process. Let them fiddle with the various features to discover what they like.

POLES

Beginning four- to six-year-olds don't need ski poles. Some children in this age group can be given poles once their ski level progresses to the point where they will benefit by them.

Ski poles are fairly inexpensive to buy, prices are usually in the $10.00 to $40.00 range. The main consideration is pole length. Make sure the pole isn't too short or long. Measure the child's ski pole as you would your own. Have the child grasp the pole under the basket with the pole's handle on the ground. If his forearm is parallel to the ground, the pole is the right length.

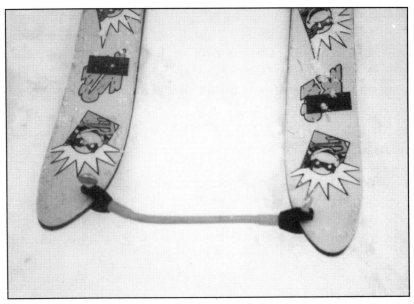

The "worm" prevents the tips of your child's skis from separating.

THE WORM

The worm is a piece of tubing that attaches to the tips of your child's skis to prevent the tips from spreading too far apart. The worm is usually about a foot long and costs around $11.00. Using a worm or similar device can greatly speed up how fast your child learns to snowplow and ski. In fact, many ski schools use them for this very reason.

EQUIPMENT BAGS

Ski bags and boot bags can be bought for junior skis and boots and are a good investment since they protect the equipment. Skis and boots for extremely young children can be transported in an adult's ski and boot bags without taking up any appreciable room.

HARNESSES

Some people use a harness while teaching to help control their child's direction and speed on the slopes. You control your child's speed by use of a leash attached to the back of their harness. Cost is around $35.00.

We do not recommend the use of a harness to teach your child. The problem is that the leash and harness tend to pull a child off her balance point. Every time you pull on the leash, you pull your child backwards, which isn't conducive to her learning balance on skis.

WAIST POUCHES

You may want to outfit your child with a small waist pouch for carrying such items as sunblock, lip balm, money, identification, and extra clothing. We saw some waist pouches designed to fit four-year-olds in a store in Aspen that were priced at $28.00. You could probably find cheaper ones elsewhere.

CRASH HELMETS

You may want to get your children crash helmets. Considering how damaging a head injury can be, it's understandable why it is now so common to see kids wearing helmets on the slopes. Providing your child with a crash helmet makes a lot of sense. Cost is in the $60.00 to $100.00 range.

As previously stated, we've often given the high end of the price range here. It is definitely possible to find less expensive equipment by shopping for sales and discount deals. Do be careful, however, that you don't buy merchandise that will fall apart when your child starts to abuse it. Generally, it's true that you get what you pay for.

4.

CLOTHING

Children's ski clothes come in as many style and color variations as adult models. In fact, some young children's ski clothing costs almost as much as that for adults (although it is possible to buy inexpensive clothing too).

SKI SUITS

Generally, one-piece jumpsuits are the warmest way to go ... while two-piece suits offer versatility. For example, your children may not always need heavy tops if they do a lot of spring skiing.

One disadvantage of a two-piece suit is that it allows snow to get into the pants when the wearer falls. The danger is that the snow then melts, making your child wet and cold. If most of your family's skiing takes place in powder-like conditions, you are probably better off putting your children in one-piece suits. Prices range from $50.00 to $200.00 for four- to six-year-olds. Older children's and teenager's ski suits range from $100.00 to $500.00.

Snow Pants

Snow pants are another good option for skiing on warm days. Price is often around $50.00 to $100.00 for young children, although it's possible to pay a lot more for older kids and teenagers. Powder pants usually have a bib that prevents snow from entering the suit. It's generally better to dress your child in ski clothes that aren't open around the waist.

Jackets/Parkas

A good quality *ski jacket* or *parka* will also be necessary if your child isn't wearing a one-piece ski suit. Ski parkas usually are longer than a standard ski jacket and cover the skier's butt as well as her upper body. If your budget is limited, buy snow pants and a ski jacket instead of the one-piece ski suit. The idea is that your child will need a ski jacket anytime he goes outside. You won't want to put your child's one-piece ski suit on every time he goes outside (such as going out to dinner). Expect to pay between $25.00 and $100.00 for a young child's ski parka.

Waterproof

Is the suit waterproof? This is an important consideration when buying a ski suit. Obviously, it doesn't make sense to save money by buying an inexpensive ski suit that allows your child's butt to get wet every time he sits in the snow. Most reputable brands are waterproof if they are designed to be used when it's snowing. Keep in mind that some stretch pants aren't waterproof since they aren't designed to be used in wet conditions. Stretch pants are, however, ideal in sunny conditions. Expect to pay between $50.00 and $100.00 for a young child's pair of quality stretch pants.

One way to make clothes waterproof is to spray them with Scotch-Guard™. Christine has a pair of snow pants that she refuses to relinquish even though they always look as though she had worn them swimming after it snowed. Spraying the pants with Scotch-Guard™ made them completely waterproof.

Tear Resistance

Make sure that all the ski clothing you buy for your children is tear resistant. It should be easy to establish whether it is since most of the major manufacturers' ski suits indicate on the label if the item is tear resistant. If a piece of ski clothing doesn't state that it is tear resistant on the label, you may want to pass. Your children are going to fall a lot while they're learning to ski ... and sliding around on cold, hard snow can shred a ski suit if it's poorly made.

LONG UNDERWEAR

If you live in an area that gets cold in the winter, you are probably already familiar with the merits of long underwear. Children's long underwear can be bought for between $5.00 and $20.00, although we recently saw some high-tech underwear for four- to six-year-olds that was priced at $35.00.

Check out the feel of the material when selecting long underwear for your children. Anything that feels rough should be avoided since you don't want their skin to become chafed. We also recommend you avoid bulky material since there are a lot of extremely thin thermal materials to choose from. Underwear that bunches up may cut off your child's circulation, resulting in his becoming cold. Also avoid underwear that has heavy seams around the wrist, ankles, or neck. Your child's ski suit will insulate these areas, not his underwear.

Long underwear can be bought in one- or two-piece designs. The one-piece design is the warmest, while the two-piece design is more convenient for visits to the bathroom. One annoying aspect of a two-piece design is the tendency of the bottom half to slip south while the top half migrates north. One solution is to get a pair of suspenders to help hold up the underwear.

GLOVES AND MITTENS

Gloves have fingers ... mittens don't. Generally, mittens are better in extremely cold conditions while gloves are more versatile. Some young children have trouble getting their fingers into gloves, making mittens the better choice. It's imperative that your child be equipped with one or the other to avoid frostbite. Gloves and mittens can cost anywhere from $5.00 to $40.00. Make sure whatever you buy is waterproof and warm in addition to being easy for your children to get their hands into.

GLASSES AND GOGGLES

It is critical that you equip your children with sunglasses or goggles. Actually, you'll probably need to buy both. Sunglasses can be worn on sunny, windless days, but goggles will be needed when it's snowing or excessively cold. Goggles are more versatile since

This helmet cost about $80.00.

This child is well-equipped to ski while it's snowing. The "Ninja" goggles cost about $17.00.

Ski goggles protect your child's eyes from falling snow and wind chill.

they can be worn in all conditions (provided they are dark enough). Sunglasses aren't adequate when it's snowing. Children's goggles cost between $10.00 and $30.00 and sunglasses cost from $10.00 to $100.00. Make sure whatever you buy offers UV protection.

SKI HATS

Ski hats come in a bewildering array of designs and colors so you may want to involve your children in selecting those that appeal to them. In fact, it's a good idea to get your children involved in selecting all their ski equipment since it will get them excited about wearing it. It's also helpful to ensure that your child is capable of manipulating the various buckles and zippers found on most ski clothing. It's better to discover that something doesn't work for your child in the store than on the ski slope.

Expect to pay between $5.00 and $30.00 for a ski hat. Hats are an essential piece of equipment and your child shouldn't ski without one. One option on warm days during spring skiing is a headband or ear warmers. A child's ears should never be left uncovered since they are particularly vulnerable and prone to frostbite.

SOCKS

The old school of thought was to wear two pairs of socks—a thinner inner sock under a heavier sock. If your child consistently states that her feet are cold, this may be still be the best way to achieve maximum warmth. However, modern ski socks are warm and well designed. You will probably find that one pair of ski socks is enough to keep your child's feet warm. Ski socks cost anywhere from $5.00 to $25.00.

SWEATERS

The key to keeping your children warm on the slopes is to dress them in layers. You will probably want to buy one or two ski sweaters to use in conjunction with your child's long underwear, ski suit, and parka. Ski sweaters can cost anywhere from $25.00 to $100.00. You may want to buy two sweaters of different weights so you will be equipped for a variety of outdoor temperatures.

AFTER-SKI BOOTS

Your children will also need shoes that can be worn in the snow when they are not skiing. A top quality pair of after-ski boots for a four-year-old can cost anywhere from $10.00 to $70.00. Older children's and teenagers' after-ski boots range in price from $15.00 to $100.00.

5.

SKILLS

To help ensure your effectiveness as an instructor, you should organize in your mind what you are going to teach your children before you arrive on the slopes. The age of the child will dictate (somewhat) the order in which you present the various skills. Four-year-olds, for example, don't need to be taught how to walk on skis during the first few lessons. Chances are you'll simply pick them up and carry them to the starting point after each run (which usually is only twenty or thirty feet long). Older children will probably be skiing with poles, and so will need to be taught how to walk, sidestep, and sideslip, along with the other basic skills that are necessary for getting around on skis.

Basically, the progression of skills is the same regardless of the child's age and is actually very simple. You will first teach your children how to snowplow and glide in a straight line. Once they have a feel for these two skills, you'll then introduce snowplow turns ... followed by stem christie turns ... and eventually parallel turns. Keep in mind that although this is a short list of skills, it may take two or three seasons of skiing before a child becomes competent at making parallel turns. Ski instruction often involves helping your children perfect what they already know. You won't necessarily always be teaching something new.

Always bear in mind the child's age and physical skills and try not to rush a youngster to the "next stage" before he or she is ready.

AGE

One of the most commonly asked questions is: "How old should my children be before they can begin learning to ski?" We suggest you wait until your children are about three and a half or four years old before you take them skiing. Naturally, there are exceptions and you will occasionally see younger children on the ski slopes. But, as a general guideline, three and a half to four is a good target age.

One of the primary reasons we don't recommend you teach children younger than three and a half is they generally don't have long enough attention spans or enough physical endurance to make ski instruction a practical activity. Taking a two-year-old out on the slopes isn't realistic. Even the ski school programs that are set up to handle children younger than four years old are really more geared toward "baby-sitting" than ski instruction (although some ski instruction is included). If you feel strongly that you want to expose a child younger than four years old to ski instruction, keep in mind that you will have to keep the lessons very short.

POLES

Children between the ages of four and seven should generally be taught to ski without poles—at least until they have mastered the basics of snowplowing and snowplow turns. Children who are eight years old or older can be given poles from lesson one. It's basically a decision based on the child's size. Taller children will need ski poles to assist them in getting around on the flats. Small children don't need ski poles since they get in the way of their learning process; small children can "skate" on the flats when there is a need.

So when should you introduce the use of poles? A good general guideline is to give your children poles when they are becoming competent in making snowplow turns. We suggest you give the children ski poles before teaching them how to make stem christie turns.

TEACHING FOUR- TO SIX-YEAR-OLDS

Teaching children in this age group is a lot of fun! You can skip teaching them the types of basics you would an older child

You can always resort to pulling your child along with your ski pole on the flats.

(such as walking, pushing themselves along with poles, etc.). Start out in an area that has a very gentle slope and is free of traffic from other skiers. You don't need to use a lift at this stage since the children will only be skiing twenty or thirty feet at a time.

We highly recommend you put a "worm" on your child's skis. As mentioned earlier, the worm is a piece of rubber tubing—about a foot long—that prevents the tips of the skis from drifting too far apart. Many young children don't have the coordination or strength to keep their skis from drifting apart when first learning to ski.

1. Squat down in front of each child and put his skis into a snowplow position. Explain to him that he should assume this position when you tell him to make "a piece of pie."

2. Next, put his skis into a straight gliding position (parallel) and instruct him to assume this position when you tell him to make "railroad tracks."

You may create other terminology for your child if you feel that "piece of pie" and "railroad tracks" aren't suitable. Spend some time going over these instructions. Tell the children to make a piece of pie ... and then railroad tracks.

FIGURE 1.

FIGURE 2.

FIGURE 3.

FIGURE 4.

3. Now stand about twenty feet in front of the children and instruct them to make "railroad tracks"—and to shuffle forward a bit to start sliding.

Ski schools often place the children on a strip of outdoor carpet (such as in these pictures shot at Snowmass) to prevent the kids from sliding forward until the instructor is ready. You probably won't want to bring a piece of carpet with you onto the slopes, but you should be able to find an area that is relatively flat with a slight hill for your child to practice on.

4. As your children begin to pick up speed, tell them to make "a piece of pie" to slow down. As they begin to slow down, follow with instructions to make "railroad tracks."

When each young skier reaches you, pick him up and carry him back to the starting point. Basically, keep repeating this drill until each child has a fairly good understanding of the transition from a snowplow to gliding straight and back again.

Once in awhile have your children snowplow to a stop. Explain to them that they can make "a piece of pie" when they want to stop.

5. After each child has become fairly comfortable with these skills you can take them onto the bunny hill or one of the area's novice slopes.

At this stage it is important to ski only on slopes that are specifically designed for children and people who are new to skiing. Naturally, you can wear your skis and ski along. Instruct them to make "a piece of pie" anytime they begin skiing too fast. You don't have to ski an entire run at this point, simply covering sixty feet or so at a time is more than adequate. The goal is to have the children begin to log some time skiing rather than standing around.

5a. Although it allows you to maintain control, holding the child between your legs prevents him from finding his own balance point.

Resist the temptation to hold the child between your legs to control direction and speed. One of the primary goals at this stage of the learning process is for the child to discover his own balance point. You'll actually slow down your child's progress if you hold him in this manner.

FIGURE 5.

FIGURE 5A.

SNOWPLOW DRILL

Use this basic exercise to develop effective stopping power with a snowplow. Having the skill to come to a complete stop while pointing straight downhill has some very practical applications; it also builds confidence.

Ski straight down the fall line with your children. Instruct them to try and flatten their skis. Point out that they are beginning to pick up speed. After a few moments, instruct them to roll their knees inward to put their skis on edge. Point out how their speed can be controlled by edging or releasing the skis. Naturally, we are assuming that the students have already mastered the basic snowplow at this point. The idea with this drill is to demonstrate how effective the snowplow is when a skier wants to control his speed while pointing straight down the fall line. A good example is to point out the ski patrol to your child when they are transporting an injured person in the sled. Show them how the ski patrol members are controlling their speed by using the snowplow.

You might also want to mention to older children that the snowplow is often the best way to ski in emergency situations. For example, if they have to accompany an injured skier down the hill who is capable of skiing, but only slowly due to an injury, the snowplow is an excellent way to control speed and to stop. You could mention that they might have to carry the other person's poles in addition to their own and that under these circumstances the snowplow is a safe way to ski.

The final step with this exercise is to have the children come to a complete stop while pointing downhill. Ski straight down the hill and come to a stop every so often by using the snowplow.

TURNING

Four- to six-year-olds generally don't understand the concept of edging skis. The best way to introduce the snowplow turn is simply to tell the child to "push" on one leg in order to turn. Exaggerate your instructions as you ski in front of your child. Say loudly, "Let's push on our left leg ... which makes us turn right." Another way to introduce turning is by playing a game called peanut butter and jelly.

Peanut Butter and Jelly

This is a fun way to teach young children "edge" awareness. It also shows them that their skis can work independently of each other.

Tell the children their left legs are used to spread the "peanut butter" and their right legs are used to spread the "jelly." The idea is to yell out "spread the peanut butter" when you want your students to edge their left skis and "spread the jelly" when you want them to edge their right skis.

This game is a useful way to demonstrate how edging a ski will initiate a turn. A lot of young children in the four- to six-year-old range seem to really enjoy this game.

It's a good idea to instruct the children to keep their hands on their knees to help them maintain balance. The concept of "pushing" the inside edge of the outside ski can often be easier to understand if the children push with both their leg and hand.

Keep Turning, Keep Turning, Keep Turning

It can be hard to convey the importance of "finishing your turns" to young children. One good way is to tell them to keep turning until they come to a complete stop—usually with their skis pointing slightly uphill. Make a turn with them following behind you and say out loud, "Keep turning ... keep turning ... keep turning," until all of you come to a complete stop. Then repeat the process in the other direction.

To help keep it fun, try alternating how wide you make the turns. Mix long sweeping turns with sharp small turns. Another way to keep things interesting is to pick "targets" somewhere on the slope around which to turn. Point out how finishing the turn helps control speed.

The above described skills will probably take up an entire season. It's much better to have your child become competent performing the skills we've outlined so far than to charge ahead into new areas prematurely. Before your children can learn to stem christie and parallel turn, they must first have a strong understanding of the basic snowplow.

TEACHING SEVEN- TO TWELVE-YEAR-OLDS

If you are teaching children younger than eight years old, chances are they won't be using poles. In this case, you should follow the same outline given in the section on four- to six-year-olds. The difference between teaching the two age groups is the terminology used. Asking a seven-year-old to make "a piece of pie" can make the child feel that you are being a little condescending. Naturally, you know how mature your child is (or feels she is). The point is, don't use the cute terms we described for young children if your child is too mature for that type of instruction.

So how should you convey the concepts of the snowplow and gliding straight to these older children? Simply stand next to the children with your skis on and show them what a snowplow looks like. Then show them the basic skiing position for going straight. Have the students ski in a straight line while you instruct them to either snowplow or glide in a straight line. It's a good idea to ski in front of the children while you give instruction so they can copy your form. For example, you can say, "Let's roll our knees in," to help the children get their skis on edge during the snowplow.

FALLING DOWN

It's important to show children that they can simply sit down if they are out of control or are in danger of hitting something. Some older kids may feel a little apprehensive about falling. Seeing you demonstrate a controlled fall will help alleviate their fears.

6. Ski in a straight line and prepare to sit down.

7. Continue to sit back and to the side.

8. Fall to the side in a controlled manner. Point out that they should keep their poles (if they have them) away from their bodies.

9. Come to a complete stop.

It's important to have your kids practice this drill one person at a time. You don't want them to slide into each other.

FIGURE 6.

FIGURE 7.

FIGURE 8.

FIGURE 9.

GETTING UP

Young children won't need to be taught how to stand up after a fall, but older kids sometimes do. If the children aren't skiing with poles, they can simply push themselves to their feet (young children have no trouble getting up in this manner). If the children are using poles, demonstrate getting up with poles.

10. Raise yourself to a sitting position with your poles in front of you.

11. Use your poles to push yourself off the ground.

12. Return to a standing position.

CHILDREN WITH POLES

If your children are big enough to use poles from the first lesson, you can show them the basics of getting around on skis.

12a. You should also show children who are using poles how to walk with skis.

12b. If your children are using poles, instruct them to hold the poles slightly forward and at about waist level.

Keep in mind that it is important to introduce these skills on a shallow slope. A child's age has nothing to do with how steep a slope they should first learn on. All novice skiers should start out on the flats.

As with the four- to six-year-olds, once the children have a good understanding of how to snowplow and glide straight, introduce the snowplow turn. With older children you may be able to actually explain to them the concept of edging a ski. If a child understands that a skier turns by putting his outside ski on its inside edge, he will always be able to make a turn (of some type) regardless of the conditions he finds himself in.

Younger children can simply be shown how to turn through example and instruction.

FIGURE 10.

FIGURE 11.

FIGURE 12.

FIGURE 12A.

FIGURE 12B.

FIGURE 13.

HERRINGBONE WALK

Teaching children to walk uphill with the herringbone walk is both a practical skill and a coordination developer.

13. Demonstrate how they can walk uphill using the herringbone walk.

KICK TURNS

This is a useful skill that also builds independent leg coordination. One word of caution: Executing a kick turn requires flexibility. If any of your children have any type of knee problems, don't encourage them to do kick turns. We also don't recommend teaching the kick turn to kids who aren't using poles.

14. Stand across the hill. Instruct your children to place their poles as pictured.

15. Lift the downhill ski as shown. (This is also a good position to use when you want to have the kids stretch.) .

16. Let the downhill ski fall across your body to the ground.

17. Lift the uphill ski and ...

18. ... bring it around 180 degrees.

19. Now you're ready to ski off in a new direction.

Explain how the kick turn can be used to change direction in difficult situations (such as on a hill that's too steep).

STEM CHRISTIE TURNS

The next skill to introduce to either age group is the stem christie turn. Four- to six-year-olds may be given poles at this point, although it's all right to wait a little longer if you feel the child isn't ready. Children seven years old and up should generally be given poles when you introduce the stem christie turn.

The best way to teach children of all age groups how to make a stem christie turn is to have them follow you in a traverse across the hill, and then instruct them to slide their uphill ski into a

FIGURE 14.

FIGURE 15

FIGURE 16.

FIGURE 17.

FIGURE 18

FIGURE 19.

snowplow position. With young children you can resort to the "peanut butter and jelly" terminology if necessary.

Once you and your students are in the half snowplow position, tell them to push on their uphill ski to initiate the turn. Remember to announce, "Keep turning, keep turning, keep turning" until you and the children have completely finished the turn. As soon as the turn is completed, bring the skis parallel to each other again.

As far as the poles are concerned, don't worry too much about pole planting at first. If your children have learned to ski without poles, they probably won't be thrilled about having to use them.

20. The first time you give your children poles, have them make snowplow turns while holding their poles slightly forward and at waist level. The idea is to get them comfortable skiing while holding the new equipment.

20a. The next step is to show them how to plant the pole and then ski around it.

Teach them to plant their poles while you lead them through a series of stem christie turns. Most children will eventually begin to use their poles naturally. It's only young children who learn to ski without their poles who may need some time to adjust.

PARALLEL TURNS

Teaching your children to parallel turn is easy if you don't try to push this skill on them too early in their skiing career. Remember that many skiers spend an entire season or two making stem christie turns. If your children are having fun, why rush things?

Chances are your children will begin making parallel turns by themselves since they are a natural extension of the stem christie.

20b. Show your children how skis are put on edge before you begin teaching them how to parallel turn.

Two important concepts to keep in mind while teaching parallel turns are: (a) encourage your children to carve their turns rather than skid, and (b) make sure you teach them the concepts of weighting and unweighting their skis. There are a few exercises and games you can use to introduce the concepts of weighting and unweighting the skis.

FIGURE 20.

FIGURE 20A

FIGURE 20B.

To begin with: Have your children bounce up and down while skiing. Point out to them that it's important to keep their weight centered over their skis, and don't let them sit back or lean forward as they go up and down. Ask them to try and "feel" how the skis respond as they weight and unweight them. Explain that as they drop their weight they are applying pressure to the skis, which pushes them into the snow. As they stand up they are releasing their skis' hold in the snow.

One way to demonstrate that the skis are unweighted is to have the children bounce up to the point of the skis actually leaving the ground an inch or so. In fact, this is an excellent exercise to use before introducing any type of "hopping" style turns commonly used on steep mogul covered runs.

Once the concept of weighting and unweighting has been introduced, demonstrate parallel turning as the children follow your line down the hill. Loudly state each phase of the turn.

"Up," as you unweight, preparing to turn.

"Pick," as you plant the pole.

"Down," as you turn.

Keep repeating the instructions as you ski down the hill and establish a rhythm.

TERRAIN—ADVANCED SKILLS

After your children have become proficient at making parallel turns—which may take several seasons—the next stage of their education is to introduce them to a variety of conditions and types of slopes. A major part of becoming an expert skier is learning how to handle different types of terrain. Powder, moguls, ice, and steep runs are just some of the many conditions that can be encountered at most resorts.

Some of the skiing styles and conditions to which you should expose your children once they have become competent at making parallel turns are:

Powder

A word of caution about skiing powder with young children. It's possible to get into powder at some resorts that is several feet deep. Clearly, this is a potentially dangerous situation for a young child who may find herself buried in snow above her head if she falls. Make sure small children understand that they shouldn't ski in the woods unless there are well established trails.

That said, skiing powder with your children is a lot of fun. Instruct them to keep their weight centered and to maintain fairly high speed. If skiers slow down in powder they tend to "bog down" since their skis stop planing. Skiing in powder is similar to water skiing. You want to maintain a fairly high speed and keep your skis planing.

It's a lot of fun to make banked turns in deep powder. Skiing powder involves a much subtler technique of lightly applying pressure to your inside edge to initiate your turn. Another point to explain to your child is that she should lead with her pole into the fall line before making a turn. We found that many children seem to suddenly "discover" how to ski powder after we demonstrate how to lead with their pole. Incidentally, if you are unfamiliar with this technique, it simply involves a slightly exaggerated downhill reach to plant the pole.

Ice

If you live or ski on the east coast of North America, you may have taught your children how to ski on fairly icy conditions. However, if your children don't have experience skiing on icy slopes, you should expose them to the technique involved. Actually, skiing on ice is an excellent way to demonstrate the importance of skiing on the edges of skis. While a child may get away with a sloppy technique on packed snow, she is in for a high speed "butt run" if she fails to edge her skis on ice. Drill in the fact that she must get her skis across the slope and on edge after every turn. In fact, you should make sure your children understand that they should *always* have their skis on edge when skiing on ice. Don't worry about explaining why ... they'll find out for themselves if they don't.

Moguls

Children love skiing on the bumps and will probably want to attack the moguls before they are ready. When you ski mogul fields with your children, point out the importance of picking out a good line. For example, ski over the top of a mogul to demonstrate a bad line ... and then ski around a few moguls to demonstrate a good line. Explain to them how they can make a series of connective turns by skiing around the bumps . . . rather than attempting to blast over the top. Conversely, show your children how they can absorb moguls by using their legs as shock absorbers. Be warned, your children are going to love skiing over the bumps. Odds are your legs will wear out before theirs.

Another important point you should explain to your children is the importance of keeping the upper body "quiet" while skiing in the bumps. Stress very little upper body movement while skiing but especially while skiing moguls. The idea is to emphasize the importance of using their legs to absorb bumps.

Chunky Snow

Skiing in clumps or sporadically spaced out piles of snow requires an exaggerated technique. One of the best ways to develop your children's skill is to take them skiing on a fairly steep hill after it has been snowing for a few days. After about half a day of use, these runs become covered with heavy clumps of snow. The only way to ski in these conditions is to exaggerate the unweighting and weighting of skis during a turn.

Find a run that is covered with heavy piles of snow and slowly ski down it with your child in tow. Loudly state, "Up, pick, plant" as the two of you ski down the run. Ski slowly in these conditions to perfect your child's form.

ATTITUDE

Many ski coaches feel that a big part of becoming an expert skier is developing an aggressive attitude on the slopes. We are not suggesting you teach your children to go out and get in fist fights while skiing, we are referring to an aggressive attitude toward the mountain.

Encourage your children to push themselves to the limit of their ability when skiing difficult terrain. Keep in mind that we are talking about children who have become fairly competent skiers.

A good way to relay the concept of attitude to your children is to suggest to them that they think of themselves as tigers. You can have fun with this. Tell them, "Let me hear you tigers roar" . . . and then roar with your children. Games such as this are a terrific way of psyching your children up before "attacking" the slope.

6.

GAMES & DRILLS

This chapter contains a collection of games and drills that you might find helpful while teaching your children to ski. As stated elsewhere in this book, one of the primary keys to keeping your children interested in their lessons is making the day fun. Introducing different games and exercises into each day's lesson plan can go a long way toward holding your child's interest.

This chapter contains games, drills, and exercises for children of all ages and ability ranges. You should be able to find a collection of exercises that will be useful for your particular teaching situation. We suggest you pick only a few of the games or exercises that you feel will be helpful to your child. Keep in mind that it's not necessary to use more than one or two games, drills, or exercises on any particular day. It's much better for your child to master one new skill than to be introduced to six and become frustrated. Conversely, there may be situations where exposing them to a wide range of activities is all that is needed to refuel their enthusiasm for the sport. The important thing is to be flexible and only use what is needed. The idea is to have countless games, drills, and exercises in your bag of tricks to call upon when the need arises, particularly if you are teaching younger children.

Some of the games, drills, and exercises we have found to be useful when teaching kids to ski are:

*Encourage your children to ski in a group when you let them
go off by themselves.*

*Tree trails are an excellent way to build
confidence and balance.*

TREE TRAILS

Skiing through tree trails (fairly narrow paths through the trees) is an excellent way to develop balance and independent leg coordination. Most ski areas have a few tree trails specifically designed for kids. You may have to ask some of the local instructors where the trails are since many of them are hard to find if you are new to the area.

If you can't find some established tree trails, you can always make your own. Don't do this with your children unless they have the ability and size to handle deep powder. The best way is for you and your friends to ski through an area a few times to establish the trail, then bring your children to the location.

The reason tree trails develop your children's skill is they are forced to edge their skis to stay on the trail. In addition, it is often necessary to absorb bumps in the trail, which helps develop leg coordination. In fact, adults often find their skiing improves from skiing these types of trails.

Use only tree trails that aren't very steep. Many tree trails traverse the mountain between slopes. Obviously, you don't want to take your children on a steep trail through trees if their ability (not to mention yours) isn't up to it.

If you are fortunate, you may discover a well-prepared tree trail complete with tunnels, pictures of animals, and other amusements designed to entertain young skiers.

DO AS I DO

As previously stated, it is a lot easier to teach young children by having them copy what you do than by attempting to explain a technique to them. "Do as I do" is simply a game where you have the children copy your movements. It will help if you slightly exaggerate what you want them to do in addition to verbalizing the action. For example, combine some of the games listed here with "Do as I do," such as announcing "I am spreading the peanut butter" as you edge your ski into a turn.

Simon Says is an excellent way to play "do as I do." For example, negative commands such as "Sit back on your skis" can be followed with positive *Simon Says* commands such as "Simon says, 'make a

Some resorts have organized "kids' trails" (such as this one at Snowmass) that go through the trees.

Practicing the snowplow!

wedge.'" The idea is to keep it fun. Ordering children to practice a particular skill may not be as effective as turning the day's exercises into a game!

FOLLOW THE LEADER

Playing *Follow the Leader* can be used to teach children how to pick a line down the slope. It's also an excellent way to practice directional control. Also, *Follow the Leader* can help control a group of children by encouraging them to ski single file. Combining *Simon Says* with *Follow the Leader* is a first-class way to encourage young skiers to copy you. The games help focus their attention on what you are doing.

SLALOM

Lay out a slalom course on a slope that is within your child's ability and have her ski it. Some ski areas often have slalom courses already laid out for recreational skiers to practice on. Once your young one has mastered the basics, she may be able to ski the resort's beginning slalom course.

Another option is to lay out a course with your ski poles or other equipment. The course can even be laid out with articles of clothing such as gloves, hats, and other small items. The goal is to have the children practice turns in addition to speed control.

Kids' Slalom is a fun variation. Place the youngsters in your class about ten feet apart in intervals down the slope. Then have the uppermost child ski the "course" ... when he reaches the last person he moves down a bit to become the bottommost "gate." Repeat the process until each child has had a chance to ski the course at least once.

You don't necessarily need a big group to play *Kids Slalom;* three individuals are enough and you can be the third.

FETCH SLALOM

You can use this game to help teach directional control. A variation is to throw a glove and then have your child ski to it and then around it. Then the child can pick up the glove and throw it down the hill, at which point you ski to the glove and repeat the game. This can be a way to create a "slalom-like" course for young skiers without having to actually lay out a course.

HOLDING HANDS

This is a game that can be used to develop independent upper and lower body coordination. Some ski instructors also occasionally have their classes hold hands to help keep the group together.

Circles is a unique game that involves holding hands. Have two young skiers hold hands while they are standing side by side and facing opposite directions. As they ski down the hill, the child facing downhill skis around his partner (who is skiing backwards) and pulls her around until they reverse positions. The idea is for the pair to ski circles around each other as they travel down the slope. This game helps develop coordination and balance.

TAG

Some children (and adults) concentrate far too hard while learning to ski. One of the things games often accomplish is taking a person's mind off his skis as he begins to think about the game. Playing "tag" can help loosen up young skiers who may be trying too hard. Make sure you don't allow children to tag each other at high speed. Even skilled skiers may attempt to collide with another child in order to tag them. Tag is best played on novice slopes where speeds won't be excessive. It is also a good idea to wear crash helmets for those accidental collisions.

SKI ON ONE LEG

One of the biggest weaknesses adult skiers have is the inability to let their legs operate independently of each other. Many intermediate adult skiers panic or lose control if one ski catches an edge. We've noticed children have the ability to develop independent leg coordination very early on while skiing. Having the ability to ski on one ski, or to unweight a ski if it hits a bump or catches an edge, isn't difficult to learn.

Have your children skate on fairly flat terrain (perhaps while

If you're working with a group, have them ski single file.

Remember, the prime objective on the slopes is to have fun!

playing follow the leader) and then instruct them to "glide" on one ski for an extended moment. Ask the kids, "Who can ski on one ski the longest?"—or—"Who can go the furthest?" Be sure you give equal time to both the left and right skis.

A variation with children who are becoming proficient with making parallel turns is to ask them to attempt to raise their inside ski off the snow a few inches as they turn. This will help ensure their weight is on their outside ski in addition to demonstrating to them how unweighted the inside ski should be.

AIRPLANE TURNS

This is an excellent way to teach body coordination while exposing kids to another method of turning. Have the children follow you over small jumps with their arms extended out to the side (like an airplane). Once in the air instruct them to turn their skis in a new direction. Kids seem to love making airplane turns while emitting airplane noises!

A simpler "airplane turn" can be made without jumping. Have your children (without their poles) ski with their arms out, airplane fashion, and then make a series of banked turns. The idea is to encourage them to ski on their edges and to roll their knees while "banking" their bodies in the opposite direction, "airplane" style. It can be very amusing to onlookers as you and your kids fly down the hill with arms extended, making your airplane turns.

LONDON BRIDGE

A fun way to help children develop directional control, speed control, and general overall balance is to play "London Bridge." Ski in front of your child with your legs far enough apart for him to ski underneath. Once he has passed "under the bridge," ski in front of him and repeat the game.

Sometimes resorting to a game like this can help you regain directional control of your child. For example, if your youngster starts skiing recklessly and chooses to ignore your instructions, you may find that he regains interest in skiing with you if you incorporate a game such as London Bridge.

JUMPING

One of the best ways you can help children develop balance on skis is to encourage them to take small jumps. Many children's ski instructors don't like the concept of encouraging children to jump since the risk of injury is slightly greater. Obviously, you shouldn't encourage your students to take jumps that are beyond their ability.

Once your children have become familiar with small bumps and seem comfortable jumping, begin to "surprise" them with jumps. The idea is to improve their skill, reaction time, and confidence by forcing them to cope with unexpected situations. Children, unlike some adults, have the marvelous ability to adapt quickly to unexpected challenges while skiing.

If you are skiing with more than one child (or person), make sure that each jump is clear before the next child goes over it. This is very important if someone falls in the jump's landing area. Recently, we saw a child fall after taking a fairly steep jump. Christine immediately advised the child to get up quickly before another skier landed on top of him. About five seconds after the child skied clear, an adult hit the jump and landed exactly where the youngster had fallen.

Another safety point to remember: Make sure your children understand that they shouldn't take any jumps if they can't see the landing area *before* they become airborne. Obviously, you don't want them to land on top of someone else.

The first few times you take your children over a small bump, it's probably best not to offer any instruction at all. Let them learn by "doing" rather than filling their heads with preconceived notions of what they should do. This especially applies to young children who will probably find their own balance point naturally. Older children and teenagers may require some instruction, particularly if they are a little timid.

Keep your instructions to a minimum. Two points that often need to be brought up are: (a) don't sit back on your skis since this can result in falling backwards, and (b) try to keep your weight centered over the skis. Generally, it's best to give advice only if you see the child really needs it.

BUNNY HOPS

This is a fun way to develop your children's strength, endurance, and ability. The idea is to have them "hop" each time they want to make a directional change.

Ski down the hill until you come to a point where you want to change directions, and then "hop" the outside ski across the fall line into the new direction ... follow immediately with the inside ski. Repeat the "bunny hop" every time you change directions as you traverse down the slope. Explaining this to your student, is difficult at best. We recommend you simply have them copy your example.

You can simplify the "hop" into a step if necessary. Simply step your ski instead of hopping. Conversely, you make the turn more challenging by hopping aggressively and limiting the amount of distance you travel between turns.

This is an excellent drill to build leg strength, confidence, and skill in the bumps. Time spent bunny hopping with your children now will really pay off when they start skiing steep, mogul-covered runs. Hopping in the above described fashion is one of the best ways to control speed on extremely steep slopes.

STEPPING DRILLS

Stepping drills are an excellent way to develop overall coordination and body conditioning. Start introducing stepping drills early in your children's skiing education.

A good one to use on flat ground is to have your children take ten rapid steps to one side and then back again. Encourage them to raise their knees fairly high to condition their legs and develop coordination. You can vary the intensity of the exercise by having them vigorously hop instead of step.

Another excellent stepping drill is to have your children step to the side as they are skiing. For example, traverse with your students across the hill and then begin stepping up the hill while you continue forward motion. A variation on this exercise is to take one or two steps up the hill followed by a 180 degree turn. Keep repeating the exercise all the way down the hill. We found this to be really effective in developing independent leg coordination.

SHADOW SLALOM

This is a fun way to encourage your children to make turns if they have a tendency to shoot downhill out of control. Ski under the chairlift and use each chair's shadow as a slalom gate. The idea is for you and your children to make a series of wide carving turns around each shadow. Kids often enjoy this game a lot.

Another advantage to this drill is it forces your children to begin to connect their turns and ski in a rhythmic fashion. It's important to instill the concept of "rhythm" into your children's skiing.

FINISH YOUR TURNS DRILL

Here's another excellent way to encourage your children to finish their turns. Instead of having them complete their turns until they come to a stop—as was previously described—have your children make a slight uphill turn at the end of each turn, and just before they begin the next turn. The idea is to have them check their speed by skiing uphill a bit prior to unweighting their skis and turning the other direction.

It can be a lot of fun and you can introduce variations into the game such as seeing which child can get the furthest uphill before each turn without losing forward momentum. Unlike the previously described drill, tell the children not to come to a complete stop after each turn.

SNOWPLOW HOP

This is a fun way to develop your children's edge awareness and independent leg coordination. Ski along in a snowplow. After pointing out how easy it is to control speed with a snowplow, instruct your students to hop sideways onto one ski ... and then to hop to the other ski after a few moments.

Have fun with the exercise and tell the children to keep hopping from ski to ski, but make sure they maintain a snowplow position. If you are skiing with older children who are using poles, instruct them to "push off" with both their pole and ski as they hop back and forth.

180-DEGREE HOP

This is a relatively advanced drill that can be used to develop coordination and conditioning. Instruct your children to stand across the slope with their skis edged to maintain their position. The first step in this drill is to have the children hop up and down so they can learn how much force is required to break their skis free from the snow. Start with single hops and then progress to several hops in a row. Point out that it is important that they edge their skis upon landing so they don't slip down the hill.

The next step is to instruct the children to try to hop 180 degrees so they are facing in the opposite direction. You can create several variations of the exercise. For example, every time you come to a stop, have the children hop 180 degrees before they begin skiing in a new direction. This is an extremely useful drill and can really pay off when your child begins to ski steep slopes, big moguls, and other advanced conditions.

ANKLE ROLLS

This is a good exercise to help your children develop edge awareness and leg coordination. You can also point out the difference between skis that are being edged and skis that are flat on the snow. Downhill racers, for example, often strive to keep their skis completely flat on the snow in order to ski as fast as possible. The moment skis are put on edge, some braking effect takes place.

Ski along with your children and instruct them to roll their ankles to the left, center, and then right. Point out how the skis respond in each of the positions. Also try the exercise with just one ankle at a time. You don't need to have them ski on one foot, simply instruct them to roll only one ankle at a time. The point is to develop your children's "feel" for how the skis respond to subtle weight shifts and pressure.

ROLLING KNEES

This is an excellent exercise to develop your children's edge awareness; it's also a good warm-up drill to loosen up the ligaments in the knees and legs.

Ski down the hill and instruct your students to gently roll their knees to the left and then the right. Point out how the skis respond when put on edge. After you've done this a few times, ask them to roll only one ski onto its edge, while the other ski is kept flat. Try the exercise with the all the weight on the edge ski and then with the weight evenly distributed. As with many of these exercises, the point is to explore the various ways skis respond to different types of physical input.

SKI ON EGGSHELLS

We don't mean that you should scatter broken eggshells all over the slopes, but asking your children to "imagine" they are skiing on eggshells is a good way for them to develop the "feel" used when skiing on crusty snow. The idea is for them to understand how to ski with a light touch rather than the usual heavy weighting and unweighting used in most conditions.

POLE-HOLDING EXERCISES

Sometimes skiers become preoccupied with how to plant their poles. Here are two drills you can use to refocus your child's attention on her skis. The following exercises can also help align a skier's body by helping her keep her shoulders facing downhill.

Tell your child to ski while holding her poles together horizontally in both hands across and in front of her body. Instruct her to keep the poles and her shoulders facing downhill as the two of you ski through a series of turns. The idea is to have your child keep her shoulders from rotating with each turn . . . a problem some novice skiers have.

The child's hand position in this exercise should be slightly higher than waist level, almost as though her hands were resting on a table.

A fun variation of this drill is to ski in pairs. Two children ski side by side while they hold onto the same long pole with both hands. The coordination required to ski in unison is an excellent skill developer and a lot of fun. Tell the children to ski parallel to each other and not to let one person move ahead. This drill can occupy kids for quite a few runs. We've seen many children who really seem to enjoy it.

BOOT TOUCH

This is an exercise sometimes used to introduce children to the concept of getting their weight forward, such as when skiing fast slalom courses.

Ski a series of turns while your children follow you. As you ski through a turn, instruct the children to lean forward and touch their boots with both hands. The idea is to have them bring their weight forward during the turn. You may find this exercise a useful way to break children of the habit of sitting back on their skis. Some kids tend to get a little lazy once they develop confidence on the slopes; they begin to sit back on their skis too much.

Boot-touching exercises are also a good way to develop overall body coordination and balance on skis. You can use the drill with new skiers as a general exercise for developing balance.

STEP TURNS

Have the children make a series of steps before a turn. The most common type of step turn involves taking an uphill step with the uphill ski before initiating the turn. Racers often use this technique to get on a better line for the next gate before making a turn.

Have your children take a step uphill with their uphill ski (followed by their downhill ski) before making a turn. Introduce them to the concept of getting on a better line before going into a new turn. For example, taking a step or two uphill before making a turn may enable a skier to avoid turning into a big mogul or a bad pile of chunky snow. Keep in mind that these stepping turns should be made "under speed." You don't want the children to come to a stop. They should take the step without any noticeable loss of forward speed.

Another type of stepping turn involves taking a step with the downhill ski *into* the turn. This is an excellent coordination builder and can also be used to get on a new line quickly.

Practicing these turns is a lot of fun. Regardless of what type of step is being taken, explain that it's equally important to push off with the other foot and to "explode" into the step prior to the turn. Naturally, this exercise should first be done at a slow speed on a low slope until the children develop the coordination necessary to execute the maneuver safely.

Here's a third exercise you may want to use to help your children develop independent leg coordination. Have them make a series of turns on a relatively flat slope by taking three or four small steps while they ski. You can use this drill with novice skiers who may benefit from the leg work. While it is possible to do the exercise on steep slopes, it's generally better to only use this game when traveling fast in the flats. The problem is the children may begin to rely on stepping turns rather than carving turns if you introduce stepping turns first.

FORWARD SIDESLIP

Here are a few fun variations on the basic sideslip that your children will probably enjoy.

Have your children traverse across the hill while simultaneously sideslipping down the hill. The idea is to get them to practice "edging" and "releasing" their skis while in forward motion. This skill also has a lot of practical application for novice skiers. If the child is traversing across the hill and wants to avoid a large mogul or clump of snow that is blocking her path, rather than stop she can simply release her edges and slide down the hill to avoid the obstacle without losing her forward momentum.

It is important that all skiers have a solid understanding of the concept of edging their skis. Remember, putting skis on edge is what makes them turn. In addition, the only way to hold your position on the slopes is to edge your skis and create a stable platform to stand on. Make sure your child understands both of these concepts. We know this sounds redundant, but most people don't seem to understand these basics. Just ask someone, "What makes skis turn." Usually, they don't know.

A variation on the sideslipping drill is to sideslip down the hill alternating forward and backward motion. You and your children should begin sideslipping down the hill while simultaneously moving in a forward direction. After you have traveled forward and down for a few feet, reverse direction and begin to slide backward. The pattern looks somewhat like a falling leaf, gently rocking back and forth as you slide down the hill.

SWIVEL HIPS

The idea of this exercise is to teach your children to alternate their weight from one ski to another. It's similar to the hopping exercise previously discussed, only the goal here is to shift the weight more than to hop back and forth.

As you ski down the mountain with the children, rapidly transfer weight from one ski to the other. Suggest that the children swivel their hips in a slightly exaggerated manner as they transfer their weight back and forth. Keep in mind, you want their hips to move, not their entire body. Pole plants in conjunction with the hip swivels can help develop coordination.

Work on establishing a steady rhythm back and forth. Watch that the children keep their poles in front of their bodies and don't allow their arms to fall behind. If their arms are falling behind, suggest that they don't actually plant their poles in the snow, but "mime" their pole plants instead.

You can expand this exercise into a series of small turns once the children have a feel for the weight transfer. While it's generally not a good idea to encourage small radius turning (because it encourages children not to finish their turns), you may want to point out how the weight transfer (and edging the ski) is enough to *initiate* a turn.

LEADING WITH THE DOWNHILL POLE

This is an excellent way to develop proper upper body form when connecting parallel turns. It's especially useful on steep or mogul-covered runs. The best way to introduce the exercise is to have your children stand across the hill and then have them rotate their bodies so they face down the fall line. Explain to them that they should reach down the fall line with their downhill pole. The idea is that once they lead with the pole the body will follow. Keep in mind that this is not a "stationary" exercise, but should be done while skiing in a series of connecting turns.

Leading with the pole is one of the most useful "visual aids" you can give your children if they are having trouble with upper body coordination on difficult runs. Many skiers tend to fall apart when they feel they are skiing a slope that is beyond their ability. The first sign of trouble is their shoulders begin to stay in line with the tips of their skis and they face whatever direction they are headed.

If you see your children falling into this pattern of skiing, there are two things you should have them do. First, slow them down. One of the most important keys to staying in control is to ski at a speed that is manageable. The second is to introduce the above drill to help realign their bodies into the fall line. Many skiers have told us that slowing down and leading with their pole has helped them get their skiing back into control.

BOX HOP

This is a fun exercise to condition the legs. You will need a cardboard box for your children to hop over.

Place the box on the ground and have the child stand next to it without his skis on. Have the child hop over the box using his poles for support. Once he has worked out the necessary coordination, suggest that he try to raise his knees as high as possible. Kids often really get a thrill out of this exercise since it's possible for them to get their legs fairly high in the air with the aid of their poles. This exercise can go a long way toward body conditioning and overall coordination.

REVERSE SNOWPLOW

Skiing backward in a reverse snowplow can be done to increase coordination on skis and to throw a little variety and fun into the day when needed. Obviously, you don't want to try this with your child on anything but a mild slope.

Ski backwards with your child with the backs of your skis close together and the tips of your skis far apart in a reverse snowplow position. Try spinning in complete circles as well as skiing backward. Point out how the skis want to naturally turn downhill if they are set flat against the snow. Get your child to experiment with different positions while skiing forward, backward, and sideways. Have fun with it.

LYING DOWN

Children do this anyway, so you might as well make a game out of it. Actually, there is a practical application to lying down on skis since it will teach your children that they can easily stand up and regain control should they fall into this position. Once again, don't encourage this activity on any but the easy-to-ski slopes.

Ski in a straight line and then instruct your children to transfer their weight back on their skis until they are actually lying flat on their backs. Make sure they understand the importance of keeping the head raised so they can see where they are going. After a few moments they should stand back up, which does require a bit of leg strength. The whole point of this exercise is to develop coordination and to teach your child that it is possible to recover from unusual body positions after a fall.

PIROUETTES

We use this to develop overall body coordination. This exercise should be done without the child wearing skis ... although it is possible to do it with skis on. Instruct the child to jump in the air and execute a 360 degree turn before landing.

The point to remember when executing pirouettes is to tell the child to "spot" the turn by turning her head before her body as she finishes the turn. Tell her to bring her head around before her body during the last half of the turn. Pirouettes can go a long way toward developing body awareness and coordination.

Have a handful of exercises that you can use when conditions aren't conducive to skiing. This way you will still be able to entertain and amuse your child if the two of you can't ski for some reason.

SPINS AND ROLLS

Freestyle skiers often incorporate various spinning and rolling maneuvers into their routines. You may want to expose your children to some of these drills to develop their coordination and ability to recover during and after a fall.

Start off with some basic tumbling exercises without the children wearing their skis or boots. You can perform shoulder rolls, back rolls, and front rolls outside in the soft snow. Explain that it's better to go with a fall and roll out of it than to stiffen and absorb the impact.

You can also expose your children to some exercises that involve rolling with their skis on. A "rollover," for example, is a freestyle move that involves first lying back on your skis, and then executing a complete roll to the side. There is some practical use to these rolling maneuvers since they show your children that it is possible to recover from a fall from a variety of positions. For example, your children can use a rollover to get back on their skis if they are sliding down the hill on their stomachs.

There is an endless variety of spins and rolls that you can show your children if you wish. Do be aware that there is a higher risk of injury when rolling around in the snow with skis on. Caution should be exercised at all times. Don't do anything your children don't have the necessary skill level and coordination for. Also make sure that there is adequate free space around each child for these exercises.

HAVE FUN

These exercises should be kept fun. Children can get a lot of enjoyment out of all these games and drills if you don't present them as hard-core skill-building exercises. Keep things light.

It is important for you to understand what the benefits are of each exercise you introduce. Children love asking "why" they have to do an exercise if they don't like it (or even if they think they *won't* like it). If you understand the goals behind the drill, you'll be able to supply them with answers to satisfy their curiosity.

Understanding the theory behind the various ski techniques you teach is equally important. If you have questions that are not answered in this book, you should seek further information. Our book entitled *The Downhill Skiing Handbook* (Betterway Books, Cincinnati, OH) is a good source of information on basic ski technique. Remember, if you don't understand what you are teaching, how can your students?

A young skier takes a breather on the slopes.

7.

RACING

COMPETITION

Some children don't enjoy physical team contact sports such as football, soccer, or basketball. Skiing gives children the opportunity to test themselves against other competitors without risking the types of injuries common to other sports that involve physical contact.

Ski racing is an excellent way for children to develop confidence, social skills, and discipline. In fact, many ski schools incorporate racing programs into their itineraries since racing has been found to be such an excellent way to develop an individual's talent on the slopes. Engaging in weekly races also provides children with a solid barometer of their skill level. Tracking their weekly times can be very rewarding since improvements can be easily seen. (If they are skiing every week, improvements in time are inevitable.)

Another advantage of ski racing for shy children is that it doesn't necessarily have to take place directly against another competitor. Some races are run against the clock, with each skier taking the course by himself. After all competitors have completed the course, the best time wins. This type of event can be an ideal way to introduce shy children to a competitive activity. While some children may be frightened by the idea of engaging in direct one-on-one competition, they may find the concept of competing against the clock less threatening. Usually as a child's confidence

*A future
Olympic racer?*

increases, he becomes more receptive to engaging in other types of competitive sports.

Incidentally, we don't feel that it's necessary for a child to take on a competitive sport to be a complete and well-balanced individual, but participation in competitive sports can be an excellent way to help some children develop socially.

Allowing your child to participate in the programs offered at most racing camps, clubs, and schools has tremendous benefits in the area of physical development. Even if your young skier is only a casual racer, she will probably get a lot of enjoyment out of all the exercise associated with these programs.

THE LITTLE LEAGUE SYNDROME

A word of caution. Over-driven parents who push their children to achieve winning times and goals beyond the children's abilities can do a lot of damage. Racing should be a fun activity for young children. Use competitive skiing to improve your child's ability and technique. If your main objective is to cultivate a future gold medalist, you are probably pushing for the wrong reasons.

Many parents have pushed so hard when it comes to competitive skiing that children who previously enjoyed the sport end up hating it. Be honest with yourself about your motivations for putting your children in a racing program. Are you doing it for them—or for you.

AGE TO BEGIN

Parents often ask when their children should be allowed to start racing. Racing can actually be divided into two categories. The first is entirely recreational, and fun should be the prime objective. All children below the age of about thirteen should be allowed to race within this loose structure of keeping it "light." Don't misunderstand us, these races are competitive events; medals won can go a long way toward building self-confidence and self-esteem. We also understand that some children will be extremely driven and have exceptional potential. Naturally, these individuals may be candidates for more serious programs at an earlier age. Most children are far better off if kept in racing programs where fun and skill building are the primary objectives. Those with the potential and drive to move on will often make that wish known.

The second category of competitive skiing is aimed toward individuals who truly have exceptional ability. Children in their early teens who want to pursue racing seriously will need to be put in racing programs that will enable them to reach their full potential. There are a number of schools, usually located near the larger ski areas, that feature ski racing as a major part of their curriculum. The Colorado Rocky Mountain College, in Carbondale, Colorado is one such school.

However, as already stated, a young racer's development—regardless of his potential—should be kept fairly non-serious until he is at least eleven or twelve. The first stage with young children is to let them compete in local weekly races such as the ones that are offered at most ski resorts.

The next stage is to join some sort of local ski club that features regularly scheduled races. There are varying levels of competition, training intensity, and a wide range of coaches and intensity of involvement at the club level of ski competition. Often, a program's seriousness is directly related to its location. Clubs situated near the big resorts, for example, often have very comprehensive racing programs and well-qualified coaches for young children. Participation is the key at this stage.

Once your children turn thirteen or fourteen years old, it's time to get them into a full-on racing program if they are serious and have exceptional talent. Keep in mind that racing starts to cost a lot in terms of both time and money at this stage of the game. You are going to pay for equipment, travel, and coaches, in addition to having other expenses to support your child's racing.

It is important to realize that a ski racer's future career options are extremely limited. Very few racers achieve any type of financial stability in their career. Even if your child becomes one of the lucky individuals who win world class events and make a living at racing ... what about his future after racing? Most coaches will tell you that only about one percent of all racers achieve any type of financial stability through their career. The point here is that you may be severely limiting your child's future options if you encourage her to pursue ski racing as her sole career. There are, however, a lot of options between total amateur and full-blown professional ski racer. Your children will probably be able to satisfy their competitive urges without sacrificing education and future options.

One other caution about encouraging your children to pursue racing as a full-time endeavor. Most professional ski racers have had at least one fairly serious injury. While recreational skiing and serious recreational racing are fairly safe, the statistics indicate that professional racing has a much higher risk of injury. We are talking about *professional* racing, not NASTAR (National Standard Ski Race) style races.

Okay, enough time spent talking about the negative aspects of letting your child pursue a professional career as a ski racer. There are basically three types of races that are run on most mountains. Slalom courses are by far the most common at the recreational and serious amateur level. Giant Slalom and Downhill are the other two types of racing to be enjoyed by your children.

SLALOM

A slalom race is essentially a race of speed with competitors skiing around a series of "gates" against the clock and each other. In the Olympics (and elsewhere) races are often won and lost by hundredths of a second. Generally, style isn't nearly as important as speed.

If you want to introduce your child to some of the basic concepts of skiing a slalom course, check if the mountain you are visiting has a slalom course set up for practice. Most mountains run NASTAR races and have one or two courses set up all the time. A note of caution: it's a good idea to only use the practice course unless you are positive that races aren't being run. Some of the basic concepts you can expose your child to are outlined below. Many of these suggestions apply to the other two types of racing as well as to Slalom racing.

Ski the Shortest Path

Explain to your children that they will ski a faster time if they cut their turns as close as possible to the slalom gates. However, don't let your children "skid" their turns in favor of carving their turns. If your youngsters are skidding around the gates, barely avoiding disaster, it's probably better to hold off on letting them ski race courses until their technique can handle it.

Incidentally, you obviously shouldn't let your children ski any slalom courses that are beyond their ability—and don't let your children ski slalom courses until they are fairly competent in making turns. The problem is that some children abandon technique completely in favor of getting down the mountain as quickly as possible. While they may log fast times, chances are they will be skiing out of control.

Tell Them to Have Fun

This is actually very important. If your children go into a race nervous, tense, and filled with fear of the outcome ... they'll probably ski poorly. Conversely, if young skiers enter a race with an attitude of "this is going to be fun," they'll most likely be much more relaxed and will ski a better race.

How a child feels going into a race has a lot to do with what mood *you* project prior to the event. If you are uptight and tense about the outcome yourself, you may well project that onto your child.

Get a Good Start

A race can be lost because of a bad start. The most common school of thought is to plant both poles in front of the body while sitting back in preparation of the start. Tell your child to think of himself as a coiled spring and to "explode" out of the gate at the end of the countdown. Instruct him to think of it as "launching" himself onto the course.

Lean into the Finish

Since races are often won by hundredths of a second, explain to the children that it is in their best interest to "trip" the clock as soon as possible. Because skis are so close to the ground, the finish line clock's "beam" often won't stop the clock until the skier's body crosses the beam. Instruct your children to lean in front of their skis with their hand to stop the clock as they cross the line.

Ski the Finish

It's important young racers don't "relax" as they approach the finish line. Explain to them that it's important to aggressively ski through the finish line to log the best time possible. One useful trick is to imagine that the finish line is actually ten or twenty feet beyond where the actual finish really is. If children use this imagery, it may help them ski aggressively through the finish.

Explain Visualization

This is helpful in all aspects of skiing, not just racing. While it may be hard for young children to understand the concept of visualization, older children and teenagers generally can apply it without much difficulty.

Explain that they should study the course and try to visualize exactly what they want to do ... and will do ... as they ski the race. You can practice visualization when you are skiing recreationally together. Instruct them to imagine how they want to look as they ski, and then have them ski a run with you while they try to let their bodies assume the image their mind is projecting. We know this sounds overly simple, but it works. Often all a skier's body needs to perform a particular skill is instructions from the skier's mind. "Instructions" can be as simple as providing a mental image of what the body should look like as it moves down the slope and through the course. Try it! You might be surprised how easily this works.

Study the Course Prior to the Race

Go over the race course with your children before they ski it. Explain to them that it will be helpful if they memorize the course rather than "discover" any sudden surprises while they ski it. Go over the distances between the gates and discuss what the best lines down the course may be. Your goal is to get the young racers to begin visualizing how they will ski their run.

Plan Ahead During the Race

Make sure they understand that they must look ahead during their run. While you, as an adult, have experience with activities that require looking ahead and planning (such as driving a car), a child doesn't. It's important for you to explain that they should plan at least two gates ahead during the race. Focusing on a gate as they ski through it is a big mistake since it doesn't allow them enough reaction time; they'll be into the next gate while they are still thinking about where they just were.

It's Okay to Fall

Explain that skiing a race with too much caution isn't a good thing. Point out that not everybody can win a particular race and that some races should be entered simply to log experience. Tell your children that it's okay if they fall. It's better that they "go for it" to find out where their limits are than to ski with extreme caution. This assumes that your child has the ability to ski slightly on the edge. A novice will naturally be more cautious than a child with a fair amount of experience.

There's No Such Thing as Failure

There's no such thing as failure—at least as far as a child entering a race is concerned. Don't promote the concept of failing with young racers. There's positively no benefit to it. Look at everything as a learning experience ... which it is. Even if your child falls at the first gate, that will teach both of you something. Perhaps they were skiing too fast or beyond their ability. Maybe they didn't have experience with the snow conditions that were present. Were they excessively nervous? Were you applying too much pre-race pressure?

Make sure that you evaluate each performance and seek to point out the positive aspects that were learned from the mistakes. Don't be a defeatist and don't let any of your children come away from a racing experience feeling that he was a failure. Developing the ability to learn from mistakes and forge ahead is a valuable skill that will benefit your children in all aspects of their lives.

Ski a Smart Race

While the saying, "speed is everything," does apply as a general rule in a slalom race, it's also important for the children to understand that skiing a smart race has benefits as well. The idea is to use some of the above-mentioned concepts such as planning ahead, looking ahead, and visualization with a general overall strategy. You want to instill in the racer that it's better to plan the race than to simply blast down the course without any strategy. Children can benefit from this concept in all aspects of their life. You'll be surprised how much children can learn through ski racing.

GIANT SLALOM

A giant slalom race is basically a long slalom. Giant slalom courses are usually skied at much faster speeds than slalom courses. While there is very little time to correct a mistake on a slalom course, a skier may be able to make up for a mistake on a giant slalom course since there is more distance between the gates. All the concepts discussed in the above section on slalom apply to giant slalom. One difference, however, is that a giant slalom course requires that your child "hang in there" mentally for a longer period of time. Pacing also becomes a factor. While a child may be able to ski "all out" on a slalom course, she will probably have to pace herself somewhat to survive the giant slalom. Generally, the giant slalom isn't skied by children at the local and recreational level. Your child probably won't encounter a giant slalom race until she becomes fairly serious about racing.

There are two concepts that apply specifically to giant slalom courses that you may wish to pass on to your child:

Stay on the Downhill Ski as Long as Possible

One of the keys to success in giant slalom is to make long carving turns. Explain that he should stay on his downhill ski until he are ready to initiate a turn in the other direction. The concept is to transfer weight from one ski to the other, eliminating the middle step used by most recreational skiers where the weight is evenly distributed on both skis between turns. In other words, a giant slalom skier is always in a state of turning.

As with all the concepts discussed in this chapter, practice carving turns and staying on the downhill ski when the two of you are skiing recreationally together.

Step Out of Each Gate with the Uphill Ski

A lot of racers use a step before they make a turn to help them line up for the next gate. The idea is to take a step with your uphill ski immediately after passing each gate ... just before you initiate a turn in the other direction. Practice taking a step before a turn when the two of you are skiing together.

This is a useful skill to develop and is a lot of fun to execute. Even if your child doesn't become involved with competitive skiing, practicing the "racer's step turn" has a lot of practical applications. It is also an excellent way for your child to develop independent leg coordination.

DOWNHILL

Downhill racing is enjoyed (unofficially) by children on a daily basis at resorts all over the world. Kids love to point their skis downhill and blast down the mountain completely out of control ... which is how some people describe downhill racing.

Downhill racing requires participants to be in top condition to survive the tremendous speeds reached during the race. Good downhill racers seem to have the ability to recover from the most amazing situations at blindingly high speeds. It is incredible to witness a racer slam into a mogul field and unexpectedly be thrown twenty feet into the air ... only to miraculously recover, land, and continue skiing the course as if nothing went wrong.

Downhill courses are clearly not intended for young skiers who do not have the ability to stay in control. Obviously, being launched into a tree at forty miles an hour isn't something any parents want to see happen to their child. It is very important that you don't encourage young racers into any skiing activity they may not be ready for.

8.

SCHOOLS & INSTRUCTORS

Although there are some disadvantages to ski schools—the primary one being cost—enrolling your child in a professionally run ski school is usually an excellent idea. In fact, if you're a tourist-type skier who only goes skiing about one week out of the year—and probably not really qualified as a teacher—then you're probably better off putting your children in ski school than teaching them yourself—at least for the first few lessons. Your kids will be off to a better start, and your relationship with them will not have suffered the frustrations of your "doing it yourself" ... when you don't quite know what your are doing.

DISADVANTAGES OF SKI SCHOOLS

Cost is the main disadvantage of ski schools. The program for four- to six-year-olds at Snowmass, Colorado costs $60.00 a day ... or $280 for five days. That can start to add up, especially if you have three or four children.

It's also possible that the ski school's program where you live (or visit) isn't very good. If you live near a ski area and are a good to expert skier yourself, you may be better qualified to teach your child than a small, under-staffed, under-trained, poorly run ski school.

Ski schools offer children the opportunity to meet other kids.

Children's ski instructors are usually fun people who enjoy teaching kids.

ADVANTAGES OF PROFESSIONAL INSTRUCTION

Quality of Instruction

Be honest about your own skiing ability. Review the questions in the first chapter. Are you really qualified to teach your child? Professional ski instructors have received years of specialized training. They also spend numerous hours each week, every month, for a good part of the year, on skis. You probably don't. If you only ski six or seven days a year, you most likely will need a refresher course yourself and should probably leave the teaching of your children to professionals.

Social Interaction

The fact that ski schools are social is another reason you may want to enroll your child. Spending the day with ten other kids gives your child the chance to make new friends, develop socially, and basically have a lot of fun. Most top-notch ski schools are well prepared and equipped to keep your child occupied on and off the slopes for an entire day.

Family Dynamics

One of the hardest aspects of teaching anything to a member of your own family is the "bicker factor." Many people can't take or give instruction to a member of their own family without getting into an argument. If you and your children have this problem on the ski slope, chances are none of you will have a good time. In fact, your children may end up disliking skiing because of all the fighting. They'll remember the fights, not the skiing. If you can't teach without an argument ... put them in ski school.

Best of Both Worlds

You may want to teach your children yourself in addition to enrolling them in ski school part time. One option may be to let the ski school teach your children the basics. You can take over their skiing education after the first few days. This will free you from having to deal with the children's first few hours on skis, which are often the most difficult and frustrating. In addition, it allows you to work out the kinks in your own technique after eleven months off of skis.

No Lift Lines

As you probably already know, ski school classes generally don't wait in lift lines. Since most young children have moderately short attention spans, there are obvious advantages to keeping them moving and out of long lines. You may also decide to take a lesson or two to get out of an afternoon of long lines.

Private Lessons Versus Group Classes

Most children do learn faster and have more fun in the group classes. While an adult may get more out of a private lesson, most children don't since their attention span is too short. Private lessons are also expensive, especially if you put your children in class for the entire day.

As previously stated, the social aspects of ski schools are a big part of the experience. Your children will most likely have a better time skiing with a group of their peers than on their own.

Group classes also give individuals the opportunity to learn from other people's mistakes. Observing other children's falls, blunders, and skiing techniques is an important part of learning to ski. In addition, the natural competitive comparisons older children tend to make about each other is healthy and is a part of the learning process that is missed with private lessons.

So why would someone want to opt for private instruction? Well, if your child has special abilities, private lessons can help cultivate these. For example, I recently skied with a four-year-old girl and a five-year-old boy of exceptional ability. Both these children had the skill, form, and look of professional ski racers. Their instructor described four-year-old Molly as "the best four-year-old in the nation"—and she looked it. With such exceptional skill, it was obviously beneficial for these youngsters to spend some time with a private instructor. However, they still played, ate, napped, and sometimes skied, with the other children in the ski school.

In addition, if your child has a special need or a disability of some type, private lessons may be the way to go. You may wish to seek out an instructor who has experience teaching children with special needs.

SELECTING A SKI SCHOOL AND AN INSTRUCTOR

One of the best ski schools we've ever seen—especially the children's program—is the one at Snowmass, Colorado. It is very apparent that the instructors at Snowmass *like teaching kids*. We asked the Snowmass Ski School Director, Victor Gerdin, how he chooses the instructors who teach the children's classes and how he brought such high quality to the Snowmass program.

Mr. Gerdin explained, "If an instructor tells us they like working with kids ... and they work as a camp counselor during the summer ... and they feel they have an aptitude for working with children ... and they enjoy it ... and they have a teaching certificate. *That's* the person I want teaching the kid's classes."

Another aspect that separates the children's program at Snowmass from many other resorts is the fact that the kids' instructors at Snowmass aren't treated as second class citizens. They're paid the same salary and have the same status as the instructors who teach the adult classes. The result is a staff made up of quality instructors who are teaching children because they choose to teach children. To quote Mr. Gerdin:

At all ski areas the private lesson instructor ends up being the prestigious position. However, at our school, if the kids' instructor has the same amount of experience as the private adult instructor, she makes the same amount of money as—if not more than—the private lesson instructor. We feel strongly that our kids' instructors are pros and we pay them as such. If someone chooses to teach children as a career, they should be as highly paid as a ski instructor can be.

The fact that instructors at Snowmass are treated well is apparent by the low turnover rate. Although there are approximately four hundred instructors on staff, only about fifteen positions open up each year.

Conversely, some of the other ski schools we talked to used the children's classes as an entry point for new instructors. It was a default position given to people who simply wanted to work at a ski area for a season, but didn't necessarily have an aptitude for teaching children. These instructors weren't paid as well as the instructors teaching adults, generally weren't trained as well, and clearly seemed less enthusiastic about their position.

How can you establish a ski school's policies and quality? Try

The well-prepared Snowmass ski school for young children even had some animals the kids could pet.

asking a couple questions. For example:

1. *Is the instructor a member of PSIA?* PSIA is an acronym for Professional Ski Instructors Of America, which is the certifying agency for ski instructors (certification is about a three-year process). Hiring an instructor who is a member of PSIA is one way of ensuring good instruction. You could also ask, "What percentage of the ski school's staff is PSIA certified?"

2. *How many hours of recertification does the staff go through each year?* Snowmass has a high standard and it shows. All the instructors on staff go through twenty hours of recertification every year. A nice touch is the fact that the instructors are paid during the four days of recertification which contributes to making the process painless. The result is a staff of instructors who are knowledgeable about *current* teaching and skiing philosophies, techniques, and equipment.

3. *Does the ski school use a teaching method?* Almost all reputable ski schools in the United States use the *American Teaching System*, which uses a logical progression of clean, simple,

easy to learn techniques. Students learn to slide, wedge (snow-plow), wedge christie, and parallel turn. The point is, the American Teaching System is a well-thought-out and time-proven method of teaching skiing. Ask what teaching method is used and pay attention to the answer. For example, we talked to an instructor in Vermont who still thought the Gradual Length Method (GLM) of teaching (popular in the late 1970s) was still "state of the art." Clearly, this person hadn't even read a ski magazine during the last fifteen years. If you ask an instructor what method she uses, and you get a "method schmethod" type answer, you should probably pass.

4. *Is the instructor associated with the ski school?* While there are some excellent independent instructors out there, you're usually better of putting your child in an organized program. All the reasons stated above about the pros and cons of private lessons apply here too. Generally, avoid independent instructors.

5. *Does the ski school provide non-skiing activities?* This question really only applies to programs dealing with four- to six-year-olds. At Snowmass, the children attend ski school for about six hours. Obviously, not all this time is spent on the slopes. Weather conditions, children's attention spans, physical and mental fatigue, and other factors all affect how much skiing can be done on any given day.

Some questions to ask before you leave your youngest ones with the instructors are: Does the school have indoor rest areas? How many breaks do they take during the day? Is there an outdoor play area? Is there an indoor play area? What happens when conditions prevent skiing? A well-run ski school should be prepared to take good care of your child all day.

Visit the ski area before enrolling your child. It should be easy to tell if the school and its instructors are well equipped and organized. When we visited the Snowmass facility, it was easy to see that they were well prepared to deal with the kids all day. The *Big Burn Snow Bears* school is centrally located, features a large outdoor fenced area adjacent to one of the main slopes, has a large indoor facility for a multitude of uses, and is well staffed. We visited other ski schools that only ran one large class, didn't provide any indoor non-skiing activities or rest areas, and were poorly staffed by under-trained instructors. You may not be able to tell much about a particular school unless you actually visit the premises. A phone interview is a useful first step, but will not give you all the information you need.

Once again, keep in mind that the above considerations apply only to ski programs for young children. Older kids, teenagers, and adults, generally don't need to be entertained off the slopes. The ski lodge and a cup of hot chocolate will usually do.

APPROPRIATE AGES FOR ENROLLMENT

Many parents wonder what age their children must be in order to be enrolled in ski school. Generally, ski schools start youngsters at about four years old. *The Big Burn Snow Bears* at Snowmass, for example, accommodates four- to six-year-olds. *The Big Burn Snow Cubs*, however, is a program designed for three-year-olds — sometimes even younger. According to Michelle Tsou-Bright, manager of both programs, Snowmass does occasionally start teaching local kids as young as two and a half, although she wouldn't recommend starting most kids that young.

Before enrolling a young child in ski school, make sure the school has a program for the child's particular age group. The age groups are usually divided as follows:

Three-Year-Olds

Sometimes younger children are admitted into these programs, but generally it's best to wait until your child is at least three or four years old. Actually, you'll probably find programs for this age group only at the bigger facilities; many resorts don't have a program for children under four. One of the reasons is teaching kids under four often involves a lot of baby-sitting, not skiing.

Four- to Six-Year-Olds

This is a fairly "standard" age grouping. Almost all of the larger and many of the smaller ski areas have established programs for juvenile skiers in this age group. In fact, we've been told by quite a few store owners that this age group is currently the fastest growing market in terms of equipment sales and development.

Seven- To Twelve-Year-Olds

All ski schools (at least the ones we've seen and/or talked to) have programs for this age group. Although this group covers children from seven to twelve, the youngsters are usually divided into groups of or near their own age. In others words, most schools try to avoid putting a seven-year-old in with a group of twelve-year-olds ... although there are naturally exceptions.

Teenagers

Don't put older teenagers in adult classes, they won't have as much fun. An adult's balance, confidence, reaction time, and physical ability aren't as good as most teenagers. Put a fearless, eager to learn teenager in a class with a bunch of scared, slowing skiing, cautious adults, and he probably won't have a good time.

Once someone is out of high school (eighteen or older), he or she can usually be put in classes with young adults in their early twenties.

9.
FIRST AID

It constantly amazes us how children can get themselves into the most outrageous, leg-twisting, painful-looking, pretzel-like positions ... only to spring to their feet unharmed and laughing. Most adults cringe when they see a child take a fall simply because they imagine the pain they would be feeling if their body parts were to become as contorted.

Skiing is basically a safe sport and children seem to be less prone to injury than adults. Nevertheless, you will probably feel more secure if you have prepared yourself to handle emergencies in the unlikely event one occurs.

The information in this chapter is presented in order to expose you to some of the basic concepts of emergency first aid. It is not a course in first aid and is not intended to replace such a class. We strongly recommend that anyone teaching skiing complete a course in emergency first aid and CPR. This is the only way you can be well prepared should your child have the misfortune of becoming injured.

CARDIOPULMONARY RESUSCITATION (CPR)

One of the first things you should learn in order to be prepared for an emergency is how to administer CPR. Many agencies offer CPR classes and most are fairly inexpensive. We have found the program at the Red Cross to be excellent. If you have to deal with a life-threatening injury on or off the ski slopes, your knowledge in CPR may make the difference between life and death. We recommend that anyone with children learn CPR.

FIRST-AID KITS

A downhill skier's first-aid kit doesn't need to be bulky. Unlike a cross-country skier, who may be miles from civilization when an accident occurs, the downhill skier is usually not far from assistance. It is still a good idea to carry a few minor items in order to be well prepared if your child becomes injured. Some of the items you may wish to carry include:

❏ Absorbent Gauze: You will find this a useful aid if you have to deal with severe bleeding.

❏ A Roll of Tape: Medical tape designed to hold gauze and bandages in place. The tape can also be used to secure splints.

❏ Various Sized Gauze Bandages: These are useful as simple bandages, but are primarily used to stop bleeding and to cover open wounds.

❏ Four-Inch Compress: Used to stop bleeding and as a dressing for a wound.

❏ A Pocket Knife: You'll use the knife to cut clothing and bandages. Folding knives are best since they don't take up much space. Having a pair of scissors built into the knife is very useful.

Carrying much more than the above-mentioned items with you isn't really necessary when downhill skiing since it is likely help will be available almost immediately. This small first-aid kit can easily be packed into the various pockets found on most ski suits. Don't burden yourself with a cumbersome pack since it's not necessary. These few items should provide for any needs you might have with unexpected emergencies.

ACCIDENT MANAGEMENT

If your child becomes injured, don't panic. Many injuries initially appear much worse than they actually are. Your first course of action is to evaluate the situation before you decide what to do. Don't rush into some action if you are unsure what type of injury has actually occurred.

Exercising accident resource management means that you should utilize all the resources you have at your disposal to deal with the situation. For example, if there are two individuals—such as you and your spouse—available to offer assistance, one of you should go for help while the other stays with the injured child. Obviously, exercising accident resource management would involve sending the better skier to get help. We know this concept sounds obvious, but its people can become quite unglued (understandably) when their child is injured.

The ski patrol at most resorts is extremely efficient and well prepared to handle all types of skiing accidents. Unless you are skiing "out of bounds" with your child—which you shouldn't be—the ski patrol will be at the accident scene within minutes. In other words, it is highly unlikely that you will have to administer any first aid yourself.

Placing skis upright in the snow in the shape of an X is the recognized sign for "help needed." If your child is injured and you are in need of assistance, take your skis off and place them in this fashion in a visible spot near the child. Teach this to your children, too.

Should you feel it necessary to leave your child and go for help, you must make sure of the following before leaving the scene:

1. *Make sure your child's life is not in immediate danger.* Life-threatening injuries such as severe bleeding, shock, and respiratory or heart failure must be dealt with immediately. Don't leave your child alone until you have established that there is no immediate danger. (Details on dealing with these injuries follow.)

2. *Make sure the child is out of harm's way.* You don't want to leave your child in an area where there is the danger of further injury. For example, if your youngster has fallen on a steep, treacherous double black diamond run, don't leave him alone if he is at risk of sliding further down the hill after you leave.

3. *Mark the location to help identify the child's location to rescue*

personnel. This serves two purposes. First, you want to ensure that another skier doesn't collide with your injured child. Second, you want to ensure that rescue personnel will be able to locate your youngster without any delay. As previously stated, crossing skis is the accepted signal for "help needed." However, a child's skis may not be long enough to be seen. If this is the case, you may opt to use a piece of bright clothing hung on one of your ski poles to mark the spot.

Keep in mind, *if you don't need to leave the victim—don't.* You can offer your child much more comfort and assistance by staying with him or her. If you stick to established runs, you shouldn't have to leave the injured child. Ski patrol will probably arrive within minutes and/or you can ask another skier to send assistance.

SHOCK

Shock is a condition that results when the body's vital organs are in a state of depression and/or the body's circulatory system is in a state of collapse. An injured person can die from shock—even if the initial injuries aren't necessarily life threatening. It's imperative you treat the person immediately when symptoms of shock are present. Symptoms include: pale and/or clammy skin—which is a result of vasoconstriction (narrowing of blood vessels and the withdrawal of the blood to the center of the body to supply warmth to vital organs), faint pulse, rapid pulse, irregular breathing (usually rapid and shallow), dilated pupils, decrease in blood pressure, and sometimes decreased kidney function. As previously stated, if action isn't taken the victim may die.

The first course of action is to treat any life-threatening injuries that may be present. Treating shock involves keeping the victim warm, calm, and lying down. A person's apprehension and fear about what is happening to her can accelerate a state of shock. Obviously, it's important that a child be comforted and that you do not allow *your* apprehension and fear about what is happening to show and frighten her even further.

Talk to your child and reassure her that she will be fine. Put her in a position that will best aid circulation (remember to first deal with possible fractures). While it may be hard to maintain warmth in the snow, do the best you can to keep her warm. Often the type of injury incurred will dictate body position. Common procedure encourages keeping the injured person flat on her back if conditions and injuries permit. Some injuries can be complicated by laying the person down—such as ones that allow fluid to enter the lungs.

DISLOCATIONS AND SPRAINS

A dislocation is a bone that has become dislocated from a joint. A sprain is an overstretched muscle, tendon, or ligament. Figuring out what type of injury your child has can be difficult without an x-ray. If you suspect your youngster has dislocated or sprained something, don't diagnose it yourself, take him to the emergency room and get an x-ray. Also, if in doubt, let the ski patrol carry him down rather than let the child ski on an injury.

Symptoms of dislocated joints and sprains include pain, discoloration, swelling, and sometimes deformity. Treating the injury involves immobilizing the affected body part (more on this later).

If your child sprains something, treat the affected area with a cold compress while elevating it. Obviously, don't let your child further exacerbate his injury by skiing or playing on the injured leg. Incidentally, sprained areas often swell so your child may not be able to wear tightly laced shoes after the accident.

FRACTURES

A fracture is a broken or cracked bone. An open fracture means part of the bone has broken the skin. A closed fracture is a broken or cracked bone that doesn't break the skin.

You may not actually see the broken bone sticking out of the victim's body. Often, the bone breaks the skin when the accident occurs and then slips back inside the body. If you see an open wound on your child, treat it as an open fracture (obviously we don't mean minor cuts, etc.). There's always a high danger of infection anytime someone has an open fracture.

If the open fracture has resulted in severe bleeding, you must prevent further blood loss (more on severe bleeding later). It's possible you may see a protruding bone in the wound—don't attempt to push it back into the body. If there is a protruding bone, gently wrap the entire wound in the cleanest cloth available. Also, wrap any bone splinters in a clean moist cloth and don't under any circumstances attempt to put them back into the body.

Symptoms of a closed fracture include pain, swelling, discoloration, and deformity. In many instances, the victim may actually hear the bone break during the accident and then feel the fractured bone parts "grating" afterwards. Naturally, if you see an obvious deformity, suspect a broken bone.

If you are faced with someone who has a broken bone, do not attempt to move him until you have immobilized the injured area. As previously stated, you are much better off waiting for the ski patrol to arrive since they are trained and well equipped to handle such emergencies. Don't try to "straighten out" a fractured arm or leg before immobilizing it—you may create further damage.

Should you find yourself in the unlikely position of having to transport an injured child off the mountain by yourself, you must first make a splint to immobilize the fractured bone. In an outdoor emergency in the snow there may be not be a lot of items available to make the splint. Ski poles can be bent to shape, skis can be strapped to injured areas, clothing (ideally blankets, which you probably won't have if you're skiing) can be folded and used to brace an injured area. Another option is to bind the injured leg or arm to the child's body. For example, a fractured arm can be secured to the chest ... a fractured leg can be secured to the healthy leg.

Keep in mind that we are talking about an emergency, no-alternatives-available situation. These drastic "makeshift" solutions should only be executed if there is absolutely, positively, no other alternative.

Splints can be fastened to the victim with tape if you have your first-aid kit with you. In the event that you do not, clothing torn into strips or belts will do a fair job. Other items that may be useful are headbands, bandanas, handkerchiefs, and the straps on your ski poles. We recommend you always carry a small pocket knife ... ideally one made in Switzerland with a blade, scissors, and a red handle. A Swiss Army Knife will be invaluable should you need to cut through clothing.

If you use hard items to make a splint—such as ski poles, etc. —place adequate padding between the splint and the child to prevent pain. Make sure the splint is long enough to immobilize the joints on each side of the fracture. Keep in mind, complete immobilization of the injured area is the goal.

Once the splint is in place, check periodically to ensure that the patient's circulation isn't being restricted. If the child says he is losing feeling in his hands or feet, for example, or the injured area starts to swell or change color, you may have to loosen the splint ties.

CAUTION: *Fractures of the back and neck are extremely dangerous since even the slightest movement may cause damage to the spinal cord (which could cause paralysis).* Do not attempt to administer treatment yourself if there is any way to contact emergency personnel. If any type of back, neck, or head injuries is suspected—even if the ski patrol is only a few moments away—*do not let the child move and do not try to move the child.*

SEVERE BLEEDING

Severe bleeding is a life-threatening condition that must be dealt with immediately. If too much blood is lost, the injured child will go into shock and may eventually die.

Apply Direct Pressure

If your child is bleeding severely, the recommended course of action is to apply direct pressure to the wound to stop the bleeding. Ideally, a large compress should be pressed against the injured area to retard blood loss. In an emergency where nothing else is available, you can apply direct pressure with your bare hands. If you are able to use a compress, do not remove it once the bleeding has stopped since the bleeding may start again. Leave it in place and let rescue personnel decide what the best course of action is when they arrive on the scene (or when you arrive at the hospital if you have to transport the victim).

Keep in mind that direct pressure can also be applied by wrapping a shirt or other piece of clothing around the wound. You may find this is ideal for serious cuts on the arms and legs.

Elevate the Wound

Elevating the injured area above the victim's heart uses gravity to help stop the bleeding. Obviously, where the child is injured will dictate the practicality of elevating the wound. Arms and legs can usually be elevated fairly easily. Keep in mind, however, that you do not want to move the victim at all if you suspect a fracture. This is especially critical with injuries to the head, neck, and spinal cord because you can seriously complicate the victim's condition by moving them. This cannot be stressed enough. It is still important, however, to stop any severe bleeding since excessive blood loss can result in death, but you can do so without risking paralysis.

Use Pressure Points

You can also stop blood loss by applying pressure to a main artery above the wound. A caution, however: by using pressure points you cut off blood flow to the entire limb, so use this technique only if both direct pressure and elevating the wound have failed to stop the bleeding.

If you must resort to using pressure points, try releasing the pressure point and applying direct pressure to the wound once the bleeding has stopped. You don't want to cut off blood flow to the rest of the limb any longer than you have to.

Tourniquet

Tourniquets are extremely dangerous and can cause the victim to lose the limb. Applying a tourniquet is a last resort and should only be done if: (a) all of the above methods have failed; (b) the victim's life is in obvious and immediate danger; and (c) there is no other course of action. Only severe life-threatening injuries, such as a severed limb, will merit the use of a tourniquet. For further information about tourniquet applications, enroll in a quality first aid course.

Not all emergencies requiring first aid associated with skiing are outward physical injuries related to falling or collision. Some serious difficulties your child may encounter include:

ALTITUDE SICKNESS

The air is thinner at higher elevations, which translates into your child's body receiving less oxygen with each breath. The higher you go, the more pronounced this problem becomes. In fact, everybody requires some period of time to adjust to the thinner atmosphere when arriving at a higher altitude.

Symptoms of altitude sickness include: shortness of breath,

dizziness, nausea, insomnia, and headaches. For most people, these symptoms pass within a few days—providing they are not trying to ski Mt. Everest. However, some individuals find the effects of altitude sickness to be so pronounced that the only remedy is to descend to a lower altitude.

Keep in mind that young children may not express altitude sickness in a manner that's easy to read. Just because you are feeling eager and are ready to ski doesn't necessarily mean your children are too. Be aware that children can be affected by altitude sickness as easily as adults.

SUNBURN

Skiing in the bright reflective snow on a sunny day is a guaranteed way to burn young sensitive skin ... or anybody's skin for that matter. It's imperative that you apply a healthy dose of sunblock to your children's exposed skin. We know this sounds obvious, but it is too often overlooked since many adults don't use sunblock themselves.

The younger the children, the more important that you put the sunblock on them since they may be incapable of doing so themselves. A young teenager can be given a tube of sunblock with instructions to apply it every few hours ... a four-year-old can't.

In addition to protecting your children's face, neck, and hands, it's also imperative to provide protection for their lips. Carmex is an excellent product to use on the lips.

Your children's eyes also run a high risk of becoming damaged if you don't protect them. A variety of goggles and sunglasses can be purchased to shield both bright light and ultraviolet light from your children's sensitive eyes. Remember, the bright conditions common on the ski slope can do irreparable damage to your children's eyes if you do not provide them with adequate protection.

Should your youngsters become the unfortunate victims of sunburn, you want to keep them indoors for a day. There are a variety of skin care products designed to heal and soothe sunburned skin.

We feel very strongly about the importance of protecting children's skin from the sun's harmful rays. Research is being released almost every day showing correlations between skin cancer and unprotected exposure to the sun.

FROSTBITE

Frostbite can be defined as the injury to body tissue that is caused by prolonged exposure to extreme cold. Young ears, noses, and faces are at high risk since they are often exposed to harsh temperatures for long periods of time on the slopes. Wind chill can greatly increase the risk of frostbite. If conditions are very cold, make sure that your children wear face masks as extra protection.

One of the biggest dangers of frostbite is that children may not know their extremities are beginning to freeze since numbness is one of the first symptoms. Children may lose feeling in their noses or ears, for example, and forget that they were previously painfully cold. Watch for symptoms of frostbite and frequently ask your children if they are cold.

The first sign that frostbite is approaching is painfully cold skin and skin that is "red-looking." If your children complain of cold skin or begin to look extremely red, take them indoors until they warm up. Obviously, it is critical to equip your children with the proper hats, gloves, face masks, and other protective equipment to ward off the cold.

If you don't take action to warm your children when the initial stages of frostbite begin to appear, their skin will continue to change color as it freezes and become grayish yellow and/or white in addition to feeling extremely cold to the touch. As previously stated, the danger is that your children may not be feeling how cold their skin is at this point.

For the record, advanced symptoms of frostbite are mental confusion, loss of sight, and eventually death. Close observation of your children will allow you to prevent frostbite from ever happening. Treatment of frostbite involves getting the children indoors and warming the affected areas. *Don't put the affected areas into hot water since this may cause tissue damage.* Also, don't attempt to warm affected skin by rubbing it to create warmth since this can also cause tissue damage. *Do* administer fluids to your child (not hot).

HYPOTHERMIA

Hypothermia is simply lower than normal body temperature. The best way to prevent your children from getting hypothermia is always to dress them appropriately for the day's conditions. Children are often more prone to hypothermia since they tend to ignore the fact that they are becoming cold if they are having fun. Part of teaching your children to ski is educating them about the dangers of exposure to extreme cold and how to safeguard against injury.

Make sure your children can recognize the early symptoms of hypothermia, which are shivering, goose bumps, and feeling cold. Children often find it interesting that shivering is caused by the body rubbing muscles together in an attempt to generate heat.

Tell children that they should go indoors and warm up when these symptoms occur. Make sure they understand that they can become seriously injured if they allow themselves to get very cold.

If allowed to run its course, advanced symptoms of hypothermia include drowsiness, mental confusion, weakness, vasoconstriction (narrowing of blood vessels and the withdrawal of the blood to the center of the body to supply warmth to vital organs), shock, and eventually death.

A child who is showing symptoms of hypothermia should be taken indoors immediately and warmed up. The same precautions outlined in the section on frostbite should be exercised here. Don't place the child in hot water and don't rub cold areas to warm them. Do make sure the child is given plenty of fluids.

10.

ODDS & ENDS

Now that you've read our book, you're ready to head for the nearest ski resort to teach your children how to ski! Before you do, here are a couple of thoughts to take with you.

DOES YOUR CHILD WANT TO LEARN TO SKI?

Does your child really want to learn to ski or do *you* want him to learn? Your child must desire to learn about skiing or all your best efforts will be in vain. Don't push skiing on a child who does not have either the interest or the desire to take up the sport. If you do, it is likely neither of you will have an enjoyable experience.

GETTING YOUR CHILDREN INTERESTED

There are a few ways you can develop your children's interest in skiing. It's often best to let them think the idea of learning to ski is theirs. If you suggest it, it may not seem as exciting as if they think they have discovered skiing by themselves. Some easy ways to get your children excited about skiing are:

Watch Skiing on TV

While you may find it hard to locate programmed skiing during certain times of the year, there is an endless variety of videos available. The Warren Miller Films are great choices because they have a modern look to them. The music is contemporary and that helps to draw the youngsters into the tape.

The idea is to let them see skiing as a young, fun, exciting activity that other young people enjoy. Avoid tapes and shows that feature a seventy-year-old Austrian instructor teaching a bunch of senior adults. Your children won't be able to relate.

Keep in mind that some children may be frightened of skiing if all they see are tapes of skiers doing extreme things on skis. This is a judgment call as only you know how your children will respond to different ideas.

Keep Ski Books and Magazines Around the House

Another great way to fuel your child's interest in skiing is to keep books and magazines around the house that feature pictures of skiing. Many skiing magazines feature annual pictorials of life on the mountain. Books that show children skiing may pique your children's curiosity about the sport.

Visit a Ski Area

You can even do this during the off season. A young child may never have seen a chair lift. Walking around a ski resort in the summer may encourage your children to ask questions about the equipment they see. Your descriptions of skiing will probably make them want to try the sport when the snow arrives.

Visiting a ski area in action can also be a great way to prime a child's interest. Seeing people ski is one of the best ways to create excitement about trying the sport.

DOES YOUR CHILD HAVE AN APTITUDE FOR SKIING?

Different people are good at different things. Some kids don't like heights, some don't like water. Some people have good eye-hand coordination while others don't. For example, my left eye is a lot stronger than my right ... which makes catching a ball difficult for me due to poor depth perception. In other words, I never was much of a baseball player as a kid.

Keep in mind that your child may have similar strong points

and weaknesses. For example, if your child has weak knees, skiing may not be for him. Don't push skiing on a child who may not have the physical aptitude for it. If your child isn't into skiing, it is not a bad thing; he will most likely find another sport he enjoys.

Some children simply don't like winter sports. Think about the adults you know. Most people are clearly either winter or summer people. Children are no different. Some kids who don't feel at home on the ski slopes may thrive at the beach.

THE OFF SEASON

Work with your children during the summer months to prepare them for the ski season. We don't mean you should put them through a daily routine of exercises, but be sure to include a healthy amount of exercise in your child's summer curriculum. What you want to avoid is going into the ski season after a half year of sedentary activity.

This is more important than you might realize. We think of children as being active, but it's surprising how much time some kids spend in front of the TV. Don't let the TV become your children's baby-sitter—get those kids outside!

You should also work at staying in shape during the off season. Family bike rides, for example, are an excellent way for the entire family to spend quality time together while getting exercise.

You can also do some exercises specifically designed to tone muscles for skiing. Some of these could include:

Sitting Against a Wall

Have your child place his back against a wall. Instruct him to move his feet out a foot or two. Now have him slide down the wall until he is in a sitting position with his back against the wall. It looks as if there is an imaginary chair under the child and the wall is the chair's back.

Count to ten (or more) and then have the child stand. Repeat the drill. This is a good way to develop the leg muscles.

CAUTION: Don't let a child do this exercise if it hurts his back or if he has a history of back ailments or injuries.

Stomach Crunches

A strong stomach is important to a skier.

Have the child lie on the floor with his knees bent and the soles of his feet on the floor. Instruct him to put his hands on each side of his head and then to flex his stomach and raise his head off the floor.

Tell him to raise up only a few inches and to look up at the ceiling or the sky. Have him do three sets of ten.

Do not allow your child to do full sit-ups; they may hurt the child's back.

CAUTION: Do not let your child do crunches or sit-ups if he has a weak back.

Push-Ups

Push-ups are a great way to build muscle in the arms in a short time. There are two ways kids can do them: on their knees, or off their hands.

Have younger children do push-ups on their knees with their knees bent. Younger children should definitely begin with knee push-ups. Aim for three sets of ten.

Keep in mind that these are only guidelines. Some children, especially older kids, may be able to do many more sit-ups and push-ups.

Stretching

Stretching can go a long ways toward preventing injuries. *You* should do a lot of stretching as well as your children. While a child's body may well be resilient and may bounce back after a fall, yours may not. If you haven't done much exercise lately, do a little stretching every other day to help loosen things up.

We recommend that you buy a book on stretching or enroll in a class to learn how to stretch without hurting yourself.

WARM UP TO THE SEASON

Make sure you give yourself a few days on the slopes without your children at the beginning of the season. It is important that you warm yourself up and get your skills back on line before you begin to teach your children. How much time you spend on the slopes by yourself depends a lot on your skiing ability. If you are an advanced skier, you may not need any practice time prior to the first lesson with your children. However, if you are relatively new to the sport, give yourself some time to get your skiing legs before you begin to teach.

TEACH SKIING ETIQUETTE

Remember to teach your children the "rules of the road" regarding skiing. For example, nothing will anger an adult skier more quickly than having a bunch of kids cut in front of him in the lift line.

It is surprising how much basic information is often overlooked. For example, some children are never told about the dangers of rocking a chair lift. Make sure you give your children the information they need to be safe on the mountain. Also teach them how to get along with other skiers. For example, spraying snow onto other skiers with hockey stops may create an unintended problem for your children if they tangle with someone humorless.

11.

CHECKLISTS

It's useful to use a checklist to help you remember everything you need to bring with you when you take your children skiing. Here's what we recommend you bring for each family member for a week-long ski vacation.

CLOTHING

☐ Long underwear—at least two pairs

☐ Socks—four to six pairs

☐ Ski suits—You can get by with one jumpsuit, but you might want to bring both a one-piece snowsuit and a two-piece warm weather outfit.

☐ Sweaters—Turtlenecks are the best choice. We suggest you bring two.

☐ Ski parka—This is for wear both on and off the mountain.

☐ Shirts—at least five. Your child can wear these both on and off the mountain.

☐ Non-skiing pants—Bring whatever your child normally wears in a week. Keep in mind that he may need a larger size to fit over the long underwear.

☐ Shoes—Bring a pair for each child to wear when playing in the snow and a pair to wear the rest of the time.

☐ Gloves—two pairs. These are essential; frostbite is nothing to fool around with.

☐ Mittens—Mittens are warmer than gloves and you may want to bring both.

☐ Ski hat—Make sure it covers the ears.

☐ Ear warmer—On warmer days, you child may be more comfortable with a head-band ear warmer. During spring skiing, for example, the temperature may be in the upper forties or warmer. However, insist on a hat on the colder days.

☐ Sunglasses — Very important. Ski areas can be dangerously bright and can damage unprotected eyes.

☐ Goggles — Protect the eyes from the sun and from damage from cold air.

☐ Sunblock—Use the highest SPF number you can find.

☐ Scarf—You may want to bring scarves for your children to use off the mountain. Don't let them wear these while skiing because of the danger of entanglement with the lift.

EQUIPMENT

You may opt to rent these items at the resort or you may rent or buy them in advance.

☐ Skis—Your child will need these!

☐ Bindings—Another obvious piece of equipment, but people have been known to buy skis and forget to buy bindings.

☐ Ski boots—Make sure that they fit correctly.

☐ Poles—These may not be necessary for younger children.

☐ The worm—Really useful for younger skiers as they learn.

SKILLS

Here is a list of the skills previously discussed. As outlined in the previous chapters, the order you teach these skills depends somewhat on the age of your child.

- ☐ Basic skiing position
- ☐ Skiing straight—The first thrill!
- ☐ Snowplow or wedge
- ☐ Snowplow turn
- ☐ Stem christie turn
- ☐ Parallel turn
- ☐ Hockey stop—Kids love this.
- ☐ Walking with skis on
- ☐ Side-stepping
- ☐ Side-slipping
- ☐ Kick turn
- ☐ Falling safely
- ☐ Getting up from a fall
- ☐ Traversing a hill

INDEX